PAST THE PAIN

PAST THE PAIN

HOW TO EMERGE FROM TRAUMA WITH PURPOSE

ANJANETTE L. YOUNG

Lawrence Hill Books
Chicago

Published by Lawrence Hill Books
An imprint of Chicago Review Press Incorporated
814 North Franklin Street
Chicago, Illinois 60610
ISBN 978-0-89733-759-5

Library of Congress Control Number: 2025947598

All images are from the author's collection

The author is represented by and this book is published in association with the literary agency of WordServe Literary Group Ltd., www.wordserveliterary.com.

Typesetting: Nord Compo

Printed in the United States of America
5 4 3 2 1

To my grandmother, Lucendia Young

You raised me with unwavering love in the heart of rural Mississippi. You were more than my guardian, you were my foundation, my guiding light. A fierce civil rights activist, a woman of deep faith, and a servant to your community, you taught me that justice, compassion, and courage are not just ideals but a way of life. Every word in this book carries your spirit, your strength, and your prayers. I am who I am because of you. This work is a reflection of your legacy.

With endless gratitude,
Anjanette

CONTENTS

FOREWORD

by Rev. Dr. Brianna K. Parker

WRITING A FOREWORD is always an honor, but in this case, it feels like sacred duty. The pages you hold tell the story of Anjanette Young—a story that is raw, painful, and courageous. It is a story that names injustice honestly, wrestles with God openly, and still insists that healing and purpose are possible.

My first encounter with Anjanette was not through headlines but in person. I had been invited to preach at her church, and she was assigned as my armor bearer. Just before worship began, she introduced herself. In that moment I realized she was the very woman whose story I had already planned to reference in my sermon. I froze. I did not want to retraumatize her by speaking about her experience without her consent. I asked her permission and even offered her the chance to hear or read it first. But Anjanette, with remarkable trust, allowed me to share it with the congregation as she heard it for the first time. That moment of trust was holy, and it prepared me for the gift of this book.

Her story begins with trauma: a wrongful police raid that left her exposed, handcuffed, and humiliated in her own home. It is a deeply personal account, but it also echoes the experiences of so many others—Black women whose safety has been disregarded, communities that have carried the weight of systemic injustice, families whose trust in "protection and service" has been shattered. The parallels to Breonna Taylor and others are not abstract; they are sobering reminders of how fragile dignity and safety can be.

To acknowledge these realities is not to turn this book into a political manifesto. It is to recognize that trauma is never only individual. It is shaped by culture, by race, by systems of power. Anjanette refuses to let us look away. But she also refuses to let trauma have the last word.

What makes *Past the Pain* extraordinary is that it moves through the valley of suffering toward the possibility of healing. Anjanette models a path that honors both faith and therapy. Her simple but profound formula—"Jesus + Therapy = Healing"—breaks silence and challenges stigma, particularly for Black women taught to carry everything alone. She reminds us that questioning God is not faithlessness but the deep faith of lament. She demonstrates that therapy is not weakness but wisdom. And she offers both tools and testimony to show that healing is possible.

The message here is universal. Few readers will face exactly what Anjanette endured, but all of us know something of loss, fear, or trauma. This book serves as both mirror and map. It reflects the weight of unhealed pain and it provides a way forward: reflection questions, professional insight, and above all the lived testimony of one who has emerged.

Her emergence does not deny the injustice. It does not erase the questions. Instead, it insists that purpose can be found on the other side of pain. That is why these pages matter. They are not only Anjanette's story; they are an invitation for all of us to sit honestly with our wounds, to seek the help we need, and to reclaim the power to live fully.

When I met Anjanette, she trusted me with her story before I spoke a word. In this book, she trusts you with her story as well. Handle it with reverence. Read it with openness. And let it move you toward healing—your own, your community's, and the healing we all long for in this broken world.

INTRODUCTION

IT'S NOT OFTEN someone can clearly look at their life before the age of fifty and say it's taken a complete 360-degree turn. But that's exactly the way I see my life's journey. I was born in Chicago, raised in the Mississippi Delta, and returned to find my purpose—even within extreme pain—in the great city of Chicago.

Let me explain more.

On a winter day in Chicago, weather was reported to be below freezing, and I entered this frigid world. It was February 26, 1970, and my mother delivered me at the historic Cook County Hospital. She was a single parent just turning nineteen who left the rural Mississippi Delta at the tail end of the Great Migration with a dream of a better life for herself and her unborn child.

What once was a dream, however, quickly became a burden. It did not take long for my mother to realize the overwhelming challenges of being a teenage single parent, trying to work and provide for little me and herself in a big, cold city.

She made ends meet for as long as she could. After realizing her best attempts to handle me in the city were not sufficient, when I was three years old, my mother traveled back to the Mississippi Delta and handed me over to my grandmother, Lucendia. My mother needed her mother's help and asked her to keep me until she could get on her feet. In fact, what began as a short-term support agreement lasted the next twenty-three years of my life.

As I'll share more in later chapters, I loved my grandmother and my childhood in Mississippi. But after completing my primary and secondary education, I too left rural Mississippi at the age of twenty-six with the same dreams as my mother: to find better opportunities in the big city. Yes, I came back to where I started. My life made a full circle. I was born in Chicago, raised in Mississippi, and later returned to Chicago.

Chicago, the third-largest city in the United States, is a mixed bag of the good, the bad, and the ugly: from world-class architecture and beautiful Lake Michigan to the negative reports of crime and corruption. However, despite its not-so-popular reviews, I eventually found my sweet spot on the Near West Side of the city, less than a mile from the beautiful downtown area with all the excitement of summer festivals, amazing skylines, and world-class culture in the museums, restaurants, and parks.

What I never imagined was that coming back to Chicago would lead to the most traumatic experience of my life. An experience that could have led to the end of my life happened just five days before my forty-ninth birthday.

Ironically, this tragic near-death experience—traumatic to its core—also set me on a new path I now know was plotted for me from the beginning. The pain I continue to endure from this event has been a part of my healing and has also led to a new purpose, not because of what happened but because of what I discovered—about myself as well as about the multi-layered and complex (un)justice system that impacts many lives, especially those of people of color. I have embraced this new purpose and share it in this book.

I invite you to embark on a journey of transformation with me as I continue to heal, serve as an advocate for those who are also healing from many types of trauma, and fight that unjust system that impacts so many. Whether you are just beginning to acknowledge the weight of your own traumatic experiences or have been searching for a way forward for years, you are not alone. The path to healing is rarely linear, but it is always worth taking.

In these pages, I will explore the nature of trauma, how it shapes us, and the many ways we can begin to reclaim our lives. You will find insights grounded in faith, redefining resilience, and practical tools to help you reconnect with your inner strength.

Over the course of this book, I will walk you through what happened to me and the subsequent fight for justice that is ongoing. But I also speak with trusted therapists and mental health professionals who give insight on not only how to heal but also how to overcome some of the obstacles in a journey involving trauma recovery.

Therapy has been one of the most valuable tools I've had the privilege of utilizing on my healing journey. It has given me the space to process my experiences, gain new perspectives, and develop practical strategies for recovery. Because of this, I wanted to integrate a therapeutic element into this book to offer readers meaningful support along the way. This is intended not to replace professional mental health support in your life but to give you a place to start or to supplement work you may already be doing.

Following each chapter, I offer a sidebar, most of which are reflections from my beloved and respected therapist Alicia Troff-Meade, a licensed clinical social worker with over forty years of clinical experience who currently operates a private practice in Oak Park, Illinois. These reflections are meant to help you unpack key therapeutic messages and apply them to your own journey. They are designed to bridge the gap between simply reading about healing and actively engaging in it.

In addition, I've included reflection questions at the end of each chapter to encourage deeper self-exploration. These questions serve as prompts to help you process your emotions, challenge limiting beliefs, and begin the important work of self-discovery and healing. I encourage you to keep a journal nearby as you read through this book so you can work through these prompts at your own pace.

Beyond the personal reflections, I have also compiled a comprehensive resource guide at the end of the book for those affected by trauma. It includes books, websites, and other content that have been instrumental in my own healing process. Whether you're looking for additional reading, professional guidance, or online communities, this list is meant to be a starting point for further exploration.

The resource guide also includes a small section for those supporting trauma survivors, whether you're a friend, family member, or professional working with individuals who have experienced trauma. My hope is that this section fosters greater understanding, encourages compassionate interactions, and ultimately helps create an environment where healing is not just possible but actively nurtured. Healing is a collective effort, and the more we learn to support one another, the more we can foster real change.

I hope this book serves as a catalyst for meaningful discussions about why we are here, embarking on the long and often challenging road of healing from trauma. This journey is not just about recovery; it is also about self-discovery, growth, and, most important, reclaiming the power to live life on your own terms, with intention and purpose.

Throughout my own journey, I have come to embrace a guiding principle that has reshaped my perspective on life. It has become my personal mantra, my North Star: "Speaking truth while living on purpose." This simple yet profound statement encapsulates the idea that while the facts of my past remain unchanged—the experiences, the struggles, and the wounds I have endured—my truth is something I actively define. My truth is how I choose to carry those experiences, how I integrate them into my life, and how I use them to forge a future that is not dictated by trauma but empowered by resilience. The same can be true for you.

Too often, we allow painful memories and past wounds to dictate our present and limit our future. But healing is about more than just surviving—it's about thriving. It's about rewriting the narratives that once confined us and instead creating a story that uplifts, empowers, and propels us forward. It is about recognizing that while we cannot change what happened to us, we can absolutely choose how we respond, how we heal, and how we move forward with intention and courage.

This book is an invitation—to acknowledge your past without being imprisoned by it, to find strength in your story, and to embrace the possibility of transformation. It is about shifting from merely existing to truly living, stepping into your own power, and defining a future that aligns with your deepest values and aspirations.

True healing happens when we reclaim the authorship of our lives. When we stop seeing ourselves solely as victims of circumstance and start seeing ourselves as the architects of our own destiny, that is when transformation begins. This journey requires honesty, vulnerability, and a willingness to confront the truth—both the truth of our experiences and the truth we choose to live by moving forward.

Ultimately, I hope these pages inspire you to not just seek healing but also to embrace the power that comes with it. I hope they encourage you to speak your truth boldly, to live your life with purpose, and to recognize that within you lies the ability to turn even the deepest pain into a force for good. Healing is not just about looking back—it's also about stepping forward into the life you were meant to live.

Healing from trauma is a central theme of this book, so let's take a moment to establish a shared understanding. Trauma has the power to make the world feel unsafe, unrecognizable, and overwhelming. It can silence our voices, chip away at our sense of self, and cast a shadow over even our brightest moments. When we endure deep pain, it distorts not only how we see ourselves but also how we engage with the world, often leaving us feeling powerless and disconnected.

Trauma is a deeply personal experience, and each person responds to it in their own way. For some, it might stem from a single event—a car accident, a sudden loss, or an act of violence.

For others, it may arise from prolonged exposure to stress, such as growing up in an unstable environment, enduring discrimination, or navigating toxic relationships. Trauma is not always a single dramatic event; it can be small, repeated moments of neglect or hurt that compound into a lasting effect in one's life over time.

When we experience trauma, our bodies and minds react in ways designed to protect us. Our natural defense mechanism sets off fight, flight, or freeze responses that help us navigate the moment. However, when the moment is over, we are left with scars that penetrate our present, and everyday activities, such as working, socializing, or even relaxing, can become overwhelming.

Trauma changes us, but it does not have to define us. The fact that you are reading these words is evidence of your courage and willingness to take a step forward.

As I open a door to give you a front row seat to my own healing journey, I want to be transparent in noting that this is not a one-size-fits-all journey. Healing looks different for everyone, and there is no right or wrong way to move forward. What matters most is that you take the first step, however small it may feel.

The journey to healing, hope, and resilience is far more complex than the world often portrays. According to the *Oxford English Dictionary*, resilience is defined as "the capacity to withstand or to recover quickly from difficulties, or toughness. The ability of something to return to its original size and shape after being compressed or deformed." Similarly, *Merriam-Webster* describes it as "the ability to recover from or adjust easily to adversity." These definitions suggest a straightforward path of recovery and return to normalcy.

However, my own healing journey has revealed a deeper truth: "Things will *not* return to their original version, as traumatic experiences shake up the world as you once knew it, but healing will allow you to lean into the recovery process. You will *not* adjust easily to adversity or change. But over time, you find your individual pace for resiliency, as it will look different for everyone." Healing is not about bouncing back unchanged or moving through adversity with ease. It is about finding a new way to navigate the world, one that honors your unique process and the growth that emerges from challenges.

My professional training as a licensed clinical social worker gives me a unique vantage point for understanding trauma, how it can leave an indelible mark on one's mind, body, and soul. I will walk you through my healing journey of "Jesus + Therapy = Healing." I will share insight on how it was important for me to both get spiritual support from my church and pastor and see my mental health therapist for trauma support. I will explore the different ways trauma shows up in life. Whether it stems from a single, shattering event or the slow accumulation of stress and adversity over time, trauma has a way of shaking us to our core. It comes unannounced, altering the course of our lives and leaving us to piece together a new reality.

My hope is that you find this book helpful in navigating the complexities of trauma and healing. Together, we will explore what it means to heal, to grow, and to rediscover the light that has always been within you. Most important, you will discover hope—the steady reminder that you are more than your pain, and healing is not only possible but well within your reach. Strap on your seat belts, as it will be a bumpy ride—healing always is! But you can emerge with a renewed sense of hope and meaningful purpose. Let's go.

1

THE NIGHT THAT CHANGED EVERYTHING

WHERE WERE YOU, God?! I screamed the words into the silence, my voice shaking with confusion, anger, and devastation. My entire body trembled as I tried to process what had just happened in my two-bedroom apartment in Chicago. It felt unreal—like a nightmare I couldn't wake up from. My mind raced, replaying the moment over and over, trying to make sense of the senseless. How could You allow this to happen to me? All my life, I prayed for protection. I trusted You to keep me safe. I believed that if I followed You, if I lived faithfully, I would be shielded from the worst kinds of pain. But now, standing here in the aftermath of something I couldn't yet fully comprehend, all I felt was abandonment. Where did I go wrong? I searched my heart for answers, for some sign that I had failed You. Had I not prayed hard enough? Had I sinned in a way I didn't realize? Was this punishment? My faith had always been my anchor, but in this moment, it felt like it was slipping through my fingers. I must have messed up big time . . . because You let this happen.

Tears streamed down my face as doubt crept into places where certainty used to live. I wanted to believe You were still there, that You still saw me, that You still cared. But all I could feel was the weight of my own brokenness—and the deafening silence that followed my cries.

My faith is my everything. With all of my heart, mind, and soul, I believe in the all-knowing and all-powerful God. I had trusted God my entire life and I knew He had been with me—from a little girl growing up through finding my way in college to a fulfilling career in one of the nation's major cities. So how could God have abandoned me during the nightmare of the evening of February 21, 2019? It was a question that would haunt me for a long time, but it was one I needed to ask in the midst of experiencing trauma. It was a question I needed in order to move past this pain and experience some healing. Questions can help us find relief in trauma—even if the answers come very slowly and in ways we just don't understand.

Prior to my real-life nightmare, I was in a really good space. At age forty-eight, I had successfully raised my Black son to adulthood in the south suburbs of Chicago—the small community of Harvey, Illinois, where I had good family support. Once he graduated from high school, I finally had the freedom to move closer to my job in the city. No longer tied to the suburbs, I could embrace a new chapter of my life and fully experience everything Chicago had to offer. The energy of the city, the diverse neighborhoods, and the endless opportunities for culture, dining, and entertainment were now within my reach. I looked forward to shorter commutes, vibrant city life, and the chance to rediscover myself in a new environment. It was a fresh start, filled with excitement, possibility, and a sense of long-awaited independence. I moved into a nice and affordable apartment just west of downtown—and less than a mile away from my job. I could walk to and from work on nice summer days with the city's beautiful skyline looming just beyond my path.

There's really nothing quite as enjoyable as summertime in Chicago, and I got to live in a great area where I could take advantage of the city's best features. At the time, I also had a great job that I loved. I was a medical social worker, and I took extra care to look after patients. I made sure they received needed care after they were discharged from the hospital—I reminded them to take their medicines, I inquired about their eating habits, and I helped them arrange services they needed for wellness. I was doing the work I was called to do: helping others. And I was just days away from my forty-ninth birthday and looking forward to my dream trip to Paris at fifty—something I had been planning for a while.

Yes, my life was good—and my relationship with God had been a big part of my realizing I had a good life. Each morning I prayed specifically for protection. As a single woman in the big city, my safety was very important to me, and I talked to God about it often—including the morning of February 21, 2019. Each time I left home, I'd pray, "Lord, cover my home; all of my doors, north, east, south, and west, from the rooftop to the basement. Keep me protected. God, protect my comings and my goings. Watch over me, keep me from hurt, harm, and danger. Dispatch angels to cover my home while I am away."

It was a Thursday, and it started as a pretty ordinary day for me. Like most days, I did my routine work at the hospital, checking on newly released patients via phone calls. Around four thirty that afternoon, I logged out of my computer and walked to a reception for the opening of the new maternal care room at the hospital, which was being held in the next building. At the reception, I chatted with a few coworkers and listened as the staff continued to talk about the hospital's great use of space for the new maternal care center. It was a big deal to have a place just for new mothers to care for themselves. After a few pleasant exchanges with coworkers and the vice presidents of the hospital, I made my way to the staff parking lot and hopped into my midnight blue Jeep Renegade, looking forward to getting home. I parked near the back of my apartment where I normally parked. Because I used this parking lot, I rarely entered through my front door. I was ready to get my Thursday night relaxation started. Shonda Rhimes's "Thank God It's Thursday" (TGIT) was my TV night. I loved *Grey's Anatomy* at 7:00 and would stay tuned to the same station all the way through *How to Get Away with Murder*, which ended at 10:00. This was the perfect way to wind down after a long week and anticipate Friday.

As I put my key in the lock at my apartment's back door, Lexi, my energetic brown and black Yorkshire terrier, greeted me with a happy dance. She needed her walk.

"All right, Lexi, I'm finally home. Let's go for that walk," I said as I threw my purse on the couch in the living room. I grabbed her leash and headed back outside through my back door. I hurriedly walked Lexi along our usual route around the block, the bright lights of the United Center, the home of the Chicago Bulls, illuminating our path. The air was crisp and the streets were quieter than usual, wrapped in the early darkness brought on by daylight saving time.

In the summer, this walk would have been bathed in golden light, but now the night arrived swiftly, casting long shadows ahead of us. Despite the change in season, our routine remained the same: Lexi trotting happily beside me while I took in the familiar sights of the city, comforted by the glow of the towering arena. We headed back inside, where I put some food and water in Lexi's bowls and went to my bedroom to undress and get comfortable.

As I pulled off my slacks and unbuttoned my blouse, I turned on my TV, thinking how happy I was that I remembered to put a bottle of wine in the fridge before I left for work. It was time to unwind and enjoy my shows. I turned my TV to ABC. I was just in time to catch Meredith Grey begin her opening monologue. But Meredith Grey's soothing and familiar voice was abruptly interrupted.

Boom! The sudden bang was so loud it shook my bedroom.

Before I could even pull myself together, I heard another boom and another one.

"Chicago Police Department! We have a search warrant!"

Still scrambling to make sense of what was happening, I bolted into my living room, my heart pounding so hard I could feel it in my throat. The only things cutting through the suffocating darkness of my apartment were the chaotic flashes of bright lights bouncing off the walls. My mind raced—*Was this real? A nightmare?* The silence was deafening, except for the frantic drum of my own pulse.

Then, in an instant, lights flooded the room, blinding me. Squinting, disoriented, I looked down—and horror shot through me. I was naked. Completely exposed. Vulnerable. My body stiffened with shock, my skin burning with humiliation and fear. I needed to cover myself. My eyes darted around the room, landing on a jacket draped over the back of my kitchen chair. Instinct took over, and I reached for it.

"PUT YOUR F**KING HANDS UP!"

The command exploded through the air so raw and furious. A deep, authoritative voice cut through the fog of my panic, and I froze. *Don't shoot me!* I screamed in my mind, so terrified I was unable to speak. The jacket slipped from my trembling fingers, pooling onto the floor. My arms shot up, and I was now unable to breathe.

Suddenly, a flood of bodies rushed into the room through the broken front door. Cops—everywhere. Guns drawn. Flashlights blinding me. Red and blue lights pulsed through the windows, casting eerie shadows across their faces. Their weapons were locked onto me, their grips steady, as if I were some kind of threat. I stood there, still completely naked, completely powerless as a dozen officers stormed my home.

I had no idea who or what they were looking for, but one thing was clear to me: I knew they had the wrong place.

I heard most of the words they were saying and the noises they were making, but they didn't make any sense.

Why in the world would the police be breaking into my house? With a search warrant? What could they possibly want in my apartment? All I ever really did was go to work and church. What could they want with me?

Even in my terror and confusion, I was struck by the utterly chaotic, unreal, and dehumanizing scene. I was naked in my normally peaceful living room with twelve strangers standing in front of me, guns drawn and flashlights shining.

I heard someone mumble something about looking for a person whose name I had never heard before.

"No one by that name has ever been here!" I shouted at the top of my lungs, fearing for my life and totally bewildered. "This is so crazy. You can ask any of my neighbors. I don't bother anybody. This is crazy. . . . You've got the wrong information. . . . My name is Anjanette Young."

The police ignored me. One cop even had a gun pointed at Lexi, who was trembling hysterically. My mind simply couldn't make sense of the situation. *What in the world was going on?*

Before I had time to process anything further, one officer yanked my arms and pulled them behind my back. *Click*. I heard the handcuffs lock, and I felt the cold steel clinch my wrists.

"Can I please call somebody?" I begged through my sobs as they opened drawers, cabinets, and closets like madmen. "I have to call somebody. This is not right. . . . You come in here and kick my door in!" My voice was shrill, filled with terror, bewilderment, and despair. I howled from my gut.

Finally, a tall, White officer spoke to me. "Get out the way and we'll explain to you what's going on," he snapped. "Just relax." He, like the others, was dressed in black tactical gear and had a bulletproof vest to protect his chest; he had a baseball cap pulled down over his head.

I hollered back. "How can I relax and I don't know what's going on?! How can you come into my house and not tell me what you're looking for?" They all ignored me. "You've got the wrong house, you've got the wrong house," I continued to sob. "This cannot be right. How is this legal?"

No one said anything else to me. It felt like a long, dreadful dream. I was standing naked and handcuffed in my own home, watching police officers dump my drawers, raid my cabinets, turn over my furniture. This nightmare was real. I was watching twelve men in dark uniforms ransack the peaceful dwelling I had worked to create, and no one explained anything to me.

This entire nightmare knocked me totally off my square in ways I still can't explain. I had done nothing wrong. I was preparing to unwind after a good day and watch my favorite TV shows. I had done nothing but try to help people as a social worker and Christian woman. *Why did this happen to me? Why hadn't God been able to stop this intrusion and interruption of my life and peace? How could this be real? How could this be my life?*

The cops finally told me there had been a misunderstanding. The head cop turned to me and mumbled, "We believe your story." He took off my handcuffs, and I sprinted to my room to get my phone.

As panic set in, my home and life in utter chaos, my mind raced for someone who could get to me quickly. Calling my family wasn't an option. They still lived in the suburb of Harvey, a forty-five-minute drive away—longer if Chicago traffic was bad.

Then, one name came to mind: Raynard "Rev. Ray" Hawkins, a pastor from my church. He was someone whom I had grown close to, a man I trusted. In that moment of fear and uncertainty, I believed he would come. He was my best chance for help, and I desperately needed it. Thankfully, he answered. But I was incoherent, sobbing and trying to talk at the same time.

Rev. Ray later recalled what he was thinking when he heard my voice on the line. "You have to understand, Anjanette is not the type of person to show dramatic emotions, so I was concerned," Rev. Ray recounted. "It was an odd time for her to call, but it wasn't super late, so I answered the call. But her voice said she was in distress. It was like deciphering gibberish. She was at a level ten with fear."

I tried to tell Rev. Ray that the police had broken into my home, but I couldn't stop sobbing. I think I heard his wife tell him to just go to my house, and I was so relieved. Someone I knew was coming to my home.

"When I arrived at Anjanette's apartment, my concern grew," Rev. Ray continued. "I saw a row of marked squad cars and they were surrounded by many, many police officers in and out of their cars. Why were there so many police cars surrounding her place? When I showed an officer my ID and told him I was from the church and this was the home of one of our members, the officer quickly said (and I'll never forget his words): 'This was a good execution of a warrant.'"

Rev. Ray thought it was an odd statement; why would that be the first thing the officer said to him? He wondered what they had done to me.

"Where is Anjanette Young?" Rev. Ray asked. The officer told him that I was inside. The reverend dashed in and found me sitting on the couch sobbing, "utterly dejected," as he later recalled. Rev. Ray asked a few questions and even made a phone call to another church member who was a police officer. He helped me settle down and stayed while maintenance from my apartment complex patched up the door that had been kicked in. Rev. Ray prayed with me and asked if I'd be OK. He asked if I wanted to come to his home and stay with him and his wife, or go somewhere else. I told him I'd rather stay at my house—although it looked a mess and I was still uncertain about the door. Looking back, I think I unconsciously knew I needed to be there to absorb what had just happened.

My broken-in front door.

While Rev. Ray prayed for me that night, I was actually pretty upset with God. I was not only confused by what had just occurred but also left wondering where God had been. I actually thought God had let me down. Hadn't I prayed for protection every day of my life—and this happened? I didn't see God in this botched raid. I really didn't see anything except those bright lights shining in my face and those strange, mean men taking over my apartment as I stood alone, scared, confused, hurt, angry, and ignored.

Sitting with Emotions (Because It's OK Not to Be OK)

After the police departed with a whispered, half-hearted apology, I was left with more than a ransacked apartment and a broken door. I can't forget the pain, the anger, the immobility, and the numbness I felt that night and many nights afterward.

Now that there is some distance from that night and I've done a lot of work toward healing from trauma, I can see things a bit more clearly, but there's no doubt that those emotions I experienced can and will at times creep up and try to take over my mind and body.

The hardest part of any healing journey is sitting in the pain. When I traveled to Israel with my church in 2017, we visited an olive orchard. I learned that the olive in its purest form is just a little green pitted fruit. But in order to get the revered olive oil that has many, varied uses, the tiny fruit must be crushed, stomped, and pressed with a grinder, which is a difficult and messy process. This is similar to the process for recovering from trauma—the crushing and pressing part hurts the most but also brings about the healing.

As Sarah Jakes Roberts notes in her book *Power Moves: Ignite Your Confidence and Become a Force*, we must endure the hard part of healing because there is beauty on the other side of our pain. She says we truly live within our purpose when we can heal from brokenness and live a life that is aligned with God's plan for our lives.

The work I've done with my therapist, Alicia Troff-Meade, whom I thankfully had been seeing for about a year before the night the police took over my place, has helped me realize the importance of recognizing those raw emotions and not running from them. I could not just tuck away this nightmare and move on with my life. There were days, weeks, and months when I touched my face and realized tears were seeping from my eyes. I cried in my bed when I couldn't sleep. I cried when I was just sitting on my couch trying to watch TV.

Trying to live a "normal" life where I focused on work, came home, and cared for Lexi and myself was a challenge. During the early days after the horrific raid, few people knew what happened to me that night. It had not yet been broadcast across the news stations, as it would be later. I had not yet been interviewed by Dave Savini, Joy Reid, Soledad O'Brien, or, later, Gayle King. I was pretty much left alone to deal with my vacillating emotions: tears, anger, doubt, disappointment, and more anger.

But looking back, one of the truest statements that helped me through that time was engraved on a rubber bracelet given to me by one of my coworkers from the hospital: IT'S OK NOT TO BE OK.

In the aftermath of trauma, it is critical to remind yourself that it's OK not to be OK. We often think we have to plaster a smile on our face and stuff down our emotions; even privately when we pray, we sometimes think we have to thank God and make a few quick requests for the day. But during this time, my prayer life essentially consisted of me asking God why He let this awful night happen to me. I truly believed in God's omniscience, omnipresence, and omnipotence—all knowing, all present, and all powerful. And I truly believed God knew what was happening. *Why didn't God intervene?* That's a question I still ruminate over when my mind wanders down memory lane or whenever a news story about a similar type of raid flashes across my TV.

Some people try to make you feel guilty for questioning God, but that's where I was, and I honestly believe it was a reflection of my deep faith. I was able to question God because I knew God's abilities. I knew what God was capable of, so I presented my honest thoughts to Him. I didn't expect a tangible answer, but I did want to understand the why, and express my feelings without the need to put a bow around them. This is how I sat with my emotions. I now can find comfort in knowing that many people in the Bible also cried out to God as they sat with their emotions. David's psalms are filled with his questioning God. In Psalm 22:1–2, David says, "My God, my God, why have you forsaken me? Why are you so far from saving me, so far from my cries of anguish? My God, I cry out by day, but you do not answer; by night, but I find no rest."

I like to think David was sitting with his emotions. It's healthy and it's OK. It's more than OK. It can be necessary when trying to recover and heal from trauma.

To accept that it is OK not to be OK means not having a formula, not even knowing how to get better, but rather honoring what you feel in the moment and letting it be. It means sitting with the emotions, whatever they may be at the time. Uncontrollable tears. Numbness. Hurt. Anger. Sadness. I was being crushed and pressed just by allowing these emotions to flow and surface. What I needed was being pressed out of me like the oil from the olive. I just didn't know it yet—I didn't know that I was making something more precious.

If you haven't given yourself permission to sit with the emotions connected to your trauma, do yourself a favor and practice just feeling. Regardless of what you've been through and how long ago it happened—the abuse, the pain, the wrong thrust upon you, the innocence stolen from you—acknowledge what you feel or felt, if you're able to name it, and sit with it. Sometimes people keep moving without stopping to think about what really happened to them, what altered their life. But we must sit with these emotions to process them.

Remind yourself that it is OK not to be OK. Healing is a process—and it often starts with acknowledging the myriad of emotions you have. This is critical, because trauma anniversaries, hearing stories similar to yours, a smell, a look, or even another simple gesture can trigger these emotions at random times in your life.

Trauma can come in many different forms and wreck your life and emotions. Common causes of trauma, according to Fort Behavioral Health, include the following:

- Physical abuse
- Sexual abuse
- Emotional abuse
- Neglect
- Witnessing violence
- Being involved in a natural disaster
- Being a victim of crime
- Serving in the military during wartime

When you are trying to deal with the effects of any kind of trauma, it can be a healing balm to sit with the emotions that arise in connection with the event and repeat *It's OK not to be OK. I'm a witness.*

What situation have you been through that has left you reeling, unable to see the reason for it? Have you, like me, questioned whether God was present in the moment? What emotions do you feel? How does acknowledging it's OK not to be OK provide comfort for you?

Advice from a Therapist

Alicia Troff-Meade, LCSW, my cherished therapist, graciously offered to expound on the tools for healing from trauma that I discuss in each chapter. Her expert advice may give you more insight into your healing journey and how to incorporate some of the practices that helped me. Of course, following the suggestions of your own mental health team is best, but I hope what Alicia says can help you too.

Alicia offers her thoughts on sitting with emotions and the value of doing so, especially after experiencing trauma:

I'd recommend that you begin by using the practice of mindfulness.

Simply observe the emotion without judgment and without distractions.

Start with observing for a short period of time to avoid overwhelming yourself.

Notice where the emotion resides in your body (stomach, head, throat, chest). When you know what part of the body is holding the emotion, find a physical description for that body part (tight, heavy, fluttery, hot, cold, breathless). Then listen for any accompanying thoughts (*I made a mistake*; *my friend doesn't care about me anymore*; *I'll never see them again*; *I'm afraid to live in my home*) and check for any desires you may have to act on the feeling (run away, criticize the other person, stay in bed, or physically attack something or someone).

Last, see if you can label the emotion. Once you've given your experience a name (sadness, anger, fear, shame), you'll find it easier to acknowledge, because it gives you a concise understanding of your perceptions and offers important information about who you are and what's happening to you. (Example: "I'm terrified that I'll be alone because I see myself as worthless.")

It is only when you understand what is happening to you emotionally that you can begin to choose what you want and set a plan to move forward.

2

THE MORNING AFTER: TAKING BABY STEPS

DURING THE NIGHTMARE of February 21, 2019, forty minutes seemed like a lifetime. As I stood there naked and baffled, scared and embarrassed, angry and bewildered, those forty minutes felt like the longest night of my life—right in my own apartment. To me, it seemed as if I was in front of these twelve strange men, naked for the majority of the time, as they ransacked my place. But the police body cam footage that we had subpoenaed—repeatedly through several Illinois Freedom of Information Act (FOIA) requests—shows that a female officer did show up and take me to my bedroom to get some clothes. This woman, Officer Ella French, spoke softly to me, and for the first time since the nightmare began, I felt like someone saw me. She told me she was going to take the handcuffs off me and let me get something to wear. She also said she would turn off her body cam so I could have some privacy getting dressed.

When I asked her what was happening, she told me she had been called to my address to assist with "getting a female dressed." She went on to say, "I am only allowed to let you get dressed and then I have to put you back in handcuffs." I was still horrified but relieved to at least get some clothes to cover my body. I was deeply grateful for her presence—it was a stark contrast to the chaos surrounding me. There was something different about her, something calming. She spoke to me with a gentleness I hadn't experienced that night, her tone carrying an unexpected sense of reassurance. Unlike the officers in my living room, clad in intimidating tactical gear, she wore a standard blue and white police uniform. That small difference made her seem less like an enforcer and more like a person. In that moment of fear and humiliation, her demeanor felt like a lifeline, offering a sliver of humanity amid the terror. (Sadly, in August 2021, this kind and respectful officer lost her life. Officer Ella French was shot and killed in the line of duty while conducting a routine traffic stop.)

A few minutes after I was able to get dressed and Officer French escorted me back to my living room, Sergeant Alex Wolinski, who seemed to be the officer in charge, appeared again. He had stepped outside and now walked back into my apartment with a different expression on his face. For the first time, he spoke calmly to me. I knew something had changed. He was so aggressive in the beginning, but now something had shifted.

"Ms. Young, we believe your story," he muttered. "I am sorry about this."

I blinked in shock. Was I hearing him correctly? I glanced around my place, which was almost unrecognizable, with furniture tossed around and my possessions strewn across the floor.

I noticed an officer putting my ironing board against my front door; he was trying to keep the door closed because they had broken it to get into my home. I had stood screaming for what seemed like hours, telling these men they had the wrong house, begging them to tell me what was happening and to just stop, and now this man was looking at me with somewhat of a sad, disappointed resolve telling me he was sorry.

That's it? You are sorry? You believe my story?

I was starring in an unbelievable movie, yet it was real. In the middle of my home, I was stripped of my rights and left gazing on the literal disregard for me and my possessions. And now this officer said he was sorry. He believed my story.

Wolinski took off my handcuffs. As I mentioned earlier, I immediately ran into my room to grab my phone, which is when I noticed it was 7:40 PM. These strange men in uniforms had been in my home for only forty minutes. They had barged into my home just forty minutes ago and changed my life forever.

What had I done to cause this? No, I didn't think I had done anything illegal or associated with the person on the warrant. I knew I was innocent of any crime. But what I did think was that I must have done something to make God angry. I had to have missed the mark with God; I had to have gone wrong somewhere on my journey. Like most victims of horrendous crimes, I questioned myself—and in some ways, I blamed myself—although I didn't even fully understand how this raid happened. I must have not been aligned with where God wanted me to be, I told myself. I had evidently done something wrong or forgotten to do something right. I didn't think my life was very sinful; I knew I wasn't perfect and there were definitely some things I could work on, but goodness, I thought I was living somewhat right and following God. I believed in God's omnipresence and omnipotence, so clearly God was able to stop this had God wanted to. My faith tells me God is in control of all things, but somehow, I—the woman who prayed nightly for God's protection and who had prayed the same prayer for most of my adult life—was left with an apartment in shambles, alone in what was once my oasis.

I cried myself to sleep that night—if sleep ever came—as I lay across my bed in the very space that now had changed my life, the space that would never feel safe again.

I called my manager at work the next morning, a Friday, and told her I couldn't come in. I also talked with another pastor of mine, Rev. Charlie Dates, the next day. He had been on a plane traveling back to Chicago the previous night, but he called me as soon as he heard from Rev. Ray that something had happened to me. Pastor Charlie said Rev. Ray just told him, "Hey doc, it's bad." I repeated to Pastor Charlie over the phone some of what happened. He heard me and prayed with me, thanking God for His protection.

Pastor Charlie says now that he was particularly struck by the fact that I was still alive. Despite the mistaken identity, the police had not pulled the triggers. They had not murdered me. The fact that although I had been violated, I had not been murdered was all Pastor Charlie could grasp, and it showed in his prayer and his words. He said God's protection was evident in my survival. The fact that he was talking to me on the phone the morning after meant I had survived. Even though I had screamed and hollered in my home with twelve men with guns drawn, I was still alive. Pastor Charlie said God had given me the strength to be resilient and forthright in my own home and had kept me alive. Pastor Charlie was so thankful for God's protection over my life that he kept saying "Thank God."

I listened to his prayer and tried to pray too, but I couldn't get past his words about God protecting me. How could we be thanking God for my protection? God didn't stop this raid. I was not protected from those twelve men breaking down my door and interrupting my life forever. I had no protection that night. That's where my mind was as I tried to figure out what to do next.

As a next step, Pastor Charlie suggested I speak with an attorney from our church, Keenan Saulter. He said, "Call Keenan. He'll know what to do."

Thankfully, I already knew Keenan, who was also a deacon, and I felt comfortable sharing some of the God-awful details of those forty minutes with him. I called him several times that Saturday, and we finally spoke, although he was out enjoying his kids' sports games. He heard the distress in my voice and knew I needed to speak with him sooner rather than later, so he asked me to stay after church on Sunday and speak with him more. I agreed.

That Sunday, I made my way to church, carrying the search warrant the officers had given me after they barged into my place and ransacked it. I needed answers, and I knew Keenan was the person to help me make sense of everything. After the service, I found him and recounted the horrific night once again, walking him through every detail. He listened carefully, his face serious as he reviewed the search warrant.

Keenan asked me a few key questions: Did I know the person named on the warrant? Had I spoken to anyone else about this incident? When I told him no, he looked me in the eye and said firmly, "From this moment forward, do not speak to anyone about this. If anyone asks, tell them I am your attorney." He handed me his card and instructed me to have anyone with questions contact him directly.

He then went on to reassure me: "We'll meet in a few days to go over everything and officially sign the contract to begin the legal process," he told me with confidence and warmth.

I took a deep breath, feeling a small wave of relief wash over me. For the first time since that traumatic night, I felt like I had someone in my corner who truly understood what needed to be done. Keenan knew exactly what he was doing, and I was grateful that he agreed to represent me. I was also thankful my pastor had pointed me in his direction.

I tried to get back to my "normal" life by the Monday after the raid. I got up as usual around 5:00 AM. I took Lexi out for a walk before work, ate breakfast, got dressed, and left home for work around 6:30. I needed my job, so I went to work, not fully understanding how this traumatic experience had impacted me emotionally and mentally. I was incapable of focusing or functioning as I usually did.

I think we sometimes believe getting back to a routine, or getting back to the normalcy of life, will help us push past the pain. We think that working on autopilot, trying not to focus on what has occurred, will somehow help us get through it and cope.

That's a Band-Aid. When you force yourself to push through that type of pain, you're burying your emotions, not dealing with them, and potentially causing even more damage to yourself physically and emotionally. Believe me, I get it: We don't know what to do in these cases. No one teaches us how to handle trauma in a healthy and whole way—if we knew, perhaps we'd be able to prevent traumatic events from happening in the first place. But that is not the case.

Historically, people—especially people of color—have been conditioned to push through and push on, no matter the pain, no matter the trauma. We have been taught, both subtly and explicitly, that strength means endurance. That resilience is measured by how well we can suppress our suffering and keep going. From an early age, we are told to "be strong," to "keep moving forward," to "not let anything break us." This message is woven into our culture, our families, and our very survival.

I thought that's exactly what I was doing that Monday morning. After everything that had happened, after the nightmare that unfolded in my own home, I forced myself to get up, get dressed, and go back to work—because isn't that what strength is? Isn't that what we're supposed to do? Keep pushing forward, no matter what?

I told myself I was reclaiming control, proving that what happened to me would not define me. That by showing up, by acting as if everything was normal, I was somehow taking back my power. But deep down, something felt off. My body was exhausted, my mind clouded, my spirit weighed down by emotions I refused to acknowledge. Still, I pressed on, convinced that stopping—pausing even for a moment to process my trauma—would be a sign of weakness.

Looking back, I realize how deeply ingrained that mindset was and how deeply hurtful it was. I wasn't truly healing; I was just surviving. And that's what we've been expected to do: survive, endure, and keep going. But at what cost? What happens when the weight of it all becomes too much to carry? I think of the countless, unnamed women and men in this world who are carrying unhealed trauma inside their bodies and their minds. What do they use to cope when they have not healed? What cost do they really pay in the long run when they haven't taken the time to process what has occurred to them?

Women of Color and Healing

Retired therapist and author Tammy Lewis Wilborn, PhD, says that Black women are less likely than other groups to seek help to heal from trauma—which can include abuse, discrimination, or even an incident like the botched raid that turned my world upside down. She says Black women receive the messages passed down to us through generations: "expectations that we are selfless, strong, silent, enduring superwomen who *should* be content with and capable of handling whatever comes our way." We think like I did: "We should be able to deal with this." So, just like I tried to do, we suck it up and keep pressing on even though inside we are slowly dying.

Not only do Black women feel they must press on, but they also are often reluctant to ask for help from others or to seek out therapy. We have been conditioned to not be a burden, says Camille Quinn, PhD, a health criminologist scholar at the University of Michigan's School of Social Work who studies the mental health equity of Black girls and women. Other women, particularly our White counterparts, are more comfortable getting help; they don't mind sharing their troubles or looking for help from others. Black women, not so much. We often have been trained not to bother other people with our stuff, so we suffer in silence. This goes beyond us wanting to be superwomen, or even strong Black women; this is about not wanting to put our issues on others. Although it comes from a place of caring and maybe some pride, we need to realize that we are worth healing and getting the help we need. All people are.

As a social worker, I know that in an ideal world, self-care is the top prescription for healthily dealing with trauma. While the details of how to actually care for yourself may differ, it's important to get the help you need when you've undergone any traumatic event or circumstance. In an ideal world, I should have been able to talk with my supervisor or manager at work and let them know what had occurred; in an ideal world, they would have suggested I take care of myself first, regardless of how much time was needed. I was in a profession that regularly deals with victims of trauma, yet truly taking the time and space to care for myself was not mentioned or even thought of. Because I was only operating on autopilot and my trauma hadn't been dealt with, my performance at work suffered. I was put on a correction action plan for ninety days, which probably cost my employer more money and time than it would have had I gotten the help I needed at that time. And I continued to struggle. I lost that job about eight months after my nightmare.

Fighting hard to get back to normal without dealing with the abnormal stuff that has occurred is like putting a Band-Aid on a gaping wound. The wound will eventually burst open again at the most inopportune time. It can even become a medical emergency. People sometimes think that keeping busy will refocus their minds and make them push past the issues.

It doesn't work. It never does.

I believe many of the medical conditions people, and especially minority women, suffer from are a result of unhealed trauma. We stuff things down, and that creates undue stress, hypertension, and deep depression. Of course, all those conditions then can lead to even worse impacts on our livelihood.

According to an article by the Mayo Clinic, "Reacting to stress in unhealthy ways can raise blood pressure and increase the risk of heart attack and stroke." It cites the following behaviors as being linked to high blood pressure (and dare I say stress, trauma, and anxiety): drinking too much alcohol or caffeine, eating unhealthy foods, eating too much, and not moving enough or exercising. The article goes on to explain that "the body releases a surge of hormones when under stress. These hormones cause the heart to beat faster and the blood vessels to narrow." This can cause high blood pressure over time, which can result in even more stress and unhealthiness.

How can we live healthy lives when we are suffering from unaddressed trauma? How can we live happy lives when our trauma is tearing up our insides, bubbling beneath the surface as we push on and pretend to be strong—all because it's what we think we're supposed to do or what we saw our mothers do? This is a traumatic cycle in and of itself.

Thankfully, I did have an outlet in place to help me start caring for myself, even before the raid. As I've mentioned, I had a relationship with my therapist, Alicia, and had been working with her for months, so I knew to call her for this emergency. Unfortunately, many people don't have a therapist on speed dial when trauma strikes.

Choosing a Therapist

In the aftermath of experiencing a traumatic incident—whatever that may be—you will cycle through many emotions. My most prominent emotions were anger and sadness, which also turned into a deep depression, disbelief, and a lot of questioning about what I had or had not done that made God forgo protecting me from this unwarranted disruption of my life. As I said earlier, I knew I needed to call my therapist, so after my pastors, my boss, and just a few other people, I called Alicia. I told her I needed to get in to see her right away. She had been a trusted therapist and a big help to me for the past two years. I had started seeing her after some professional challenges; for some reason, I was struggling to pass some exams that would take me to a new level in my career. I didn't know why I couldn't pass these exams when I was confident in my work. So, after months of struggling, I had sought professional help to dig into my inner thoughts and emotions to see if the struggles stemmed from something I hadn't considered.

I need to be transparent and let you know that finding the right therapist for me was not an easy job. It too took work, which is often problematic when you're trying to find one immediately after a traumatic experience. Before landing with Alicia, I tried two other counselors. I went through my health insurance's employee assistance program, where I could select therapists in their network and insurance would pay for the first few visits. This is an often-unused benefit—many people don't know about it, and when they do know about it, it still takes extra effort to utilize. I knew about these resources because of the nature of my work, and it still took me time and energy to access them.

What should you prioritize when searching for a therapist? In my case, when I looked through the directory of the professionals under my insurance's program, I made a short list of needs. I wanted to speak with a woman, because I thought a woman might understand me best. After seeing the first two women, I knew they were not the fit for me. I was mid-career, and they were noticeably younger than me.

I just didn't think they'd be able to help me with where I was professionally and personally.

I also didn't want to travel too far to see my therapist, especially since this was before the pandemic, when telehealth wasn't prominent. Traveling to see a therapist wouldn't fit into my schedule. I needed to make my visit convenient for me, so I also searched by zip code.

Let me pause a moment and acknowledge other barriers to seeing a therapist, which I fully understand and am sensitive to, even when suggesting people break through those barriers and get the help they need. In some communities—like my community, the African American community—the concept of therapy can be controversial. Thank God more and more people are opening up about their positive experiences in therapy, but it has been known as an elite choice reserved for those with extra resources or even those who may have a severe psychotic disorder. For everyday people trying to navigate through life—regardless of their trials and tribulations—therapy has just not been viewed as a natural and healthy choice. We have been conditioned to keep family business inside the house. Even within families, some things are just not discussed. Even as Christians, we say go to God; pray about it; don't share your business with outsiders.

When dealing with these barriers, it can be helpful to understand what therapy really is. Dr. Tammy Lewis Wilborn tells me: "Therapy is a professional relationship intended for you to experience change and growth and healing." She emphasizes the word *professional*. "Oftentimes we've talked with people who love us—mom, cousin . . . people you have a personal relationship with." However, the people in *personal* relationships come with opinions and, sometimes, shame. What they offer may give temporary relief, but a professional therapist has "a responsibility to understand what you are seeking from a counseling relationship and work with you on those goals. . . . Therapy can be a safe place and a soft landing spot for you to really do that work."

I knew I needed therapy, and I landed in the office of Alicia, a licensed clinical social worker who had an office in a west suburb close to my home and work. After having gone to two different therapists, I finally felt comfortable talking with Alicia. I originally wanted to find a Black woman therapist, someone whom I could identify with. As Wilborn notes, Black women can find comfort in working with other Black women as their therapist because they don't have to explain being Black and female before they even get to the issue they need to discuss in therapy.

Initially, I felt that way too, but when those first two younger women (who were not Black either) didn't work out, I tried Alicia. She was older than I was and had the amount of professional experience I needed. I also felt very comfortable with her. I had to have a hard talk with myself about my needs when deciding on my therapist. At that point in my life and for what I was dealing with professionally, I believe the therapist's age and experience were more important. I needed someone I could identify with more on a professional level than through my experiences as a Black woman. I was professionally in mid-career and also someone who worked in the field. I knew how to talk as a clinician and as a client advocate; I needed a professional who was strong and confident in their work to know how to break through that persona and get to the center of my thoughts and emotions. I have a strong personality, and I could easily step in and be the expert in that space, but I needed to be the client. I needed to be vulnerable enough to deal with the issues and let my therapist advise me. Among the therapists I had tried and was exposed to, Alicia best fit that mode for me. I'm happy I did the hard work of asking myself to prioritize my needs.

Understanding your needs can help you when searching for a therapist. Also recognize that you may need to find a different therapist as your needs change. It's OK. Be honest with yourself; ask yourself questions and keep track of how you feel with each therapist you try.

Wilborn suggests you consider your immediate needs. Do you need someone who can help with issues around family like relationship conflicts, divorce or separation, family trauma, or problems with a child? Or do you need someone to help with personal issues, such as depression or trauma? Or perhaps you're having a work-related issue and need someone to talk with about those issues. Identifying your needs is a critical first step.

Wilborn tells me that you might have to "date" a few therapists before you find the right one. Just because you've taken the very important step to see one doesn't necessarily mean that the first therapist you visit will be the right one. "Do a little digging, meet with a couple of folks before you meet the right one—but know that there is a right one out there. Keep trying. You are worth it!" she affirms.

I also let Alicia know how important my faith is to me. I didn't want her trying to talk away my belief in God. While not self-identified as a Christian therapist, she said she understood my faith was important. She has demonstrated her care and concern for my faith as she has walked with me through my healing journey. We even read a Christian book together to assist in my processing of my feelings and to push me toward healing. (I've included that book and others in the resource guide in the back of this book.)

When you are looking for a therapist, ask yourself what is most important to you: gender, race, belief system, approach. Ask around to see if anyone you know has recommendations, and most important, as Wilborn reiterates, don't be afraid to find a new therapist when you feel the fit isn't right. This person will hopefully be one of the contributing forces in your recovery from trauma as well as your finding and re-finding wholeness and health. While it may feel inconvenient to have to search for a new therapist, it could make a difference in your healing. You want the right fit, or someone with whom you feel totally comfortable sharing some of your most personal inner feelings. Your therapist will probably help you uncover things you didn't even know were inside of you—you can't trust that to just anyone. And you probably won't be able to uncover those depths with someone you don't trust or can't be vulnerable with.

Wilborn also points out that there are different types of therapists to help you work through different needs; there are some who are trained in trauma healing or domestic issues. She lists many different types and offers helpful guidance on finding the right fit in her book *Playing a New Game: A Black Woman's Guide to Being Well and Thriving in the Workplace.*

One of the easiest ways to identify a therapist is to get recommendations from friends, family members, or even your primary care physician or another doctor. You can also ask for a list from your insurance company, especially if you are utilizing health benefits to minimize out-of-pocket costs. There are directories you can search according to specialties and locations. Consider sites like Psychology Today (https://www.psychologytoday.com), Therapy for Black Girls (https://therapyforblackgirls.com/), and Clinicians of Color (https://www.cliniciansofcolor.org/). See the resources section for more information on finding a therapist.

Regardless of where you land with a therapist, Wilborn reminds us that it is important to show up. "Remember, the first thing is your wellness and your well-being matters; you've got to believe that. You've got to believe it matters.

"Therapy is important because the things that have happened to us will tell us we don't matter, that we're not enough . . . and all of these different messages become the tape in our head. You need to eject that tape and say, 'my well-being matters.'"

Talk with a Therapist

During the first two years when I visited Alicia—before my encounter with the Chicago Police Department—she asked me, "You look like you want to cry but you don't cry. Why do you feel you can't cry?"

I remember her words challenging me to think about my beliefs. At the time, I thought both my faith and my upbringing taught me to be strong. I grew up in an environment where pushing through adversity was not just encouraged but expected. It became second nature to me—to never let things bring me down, to keep moving forward no matter the challenge. Growing up in rural Mississippi, I learned early on that racism wasn't something hidden, it was a harsh reality that shaped my world. I understood the unspoken rule: I had to stay on "our side of the tracks." And I had to be strong.

Navigating my way through life, from the small town I called home to the larger, more complex world of college and beyond, I carried that mentality with me. Whether it was balancing the pressures of higher education, raising a family, or climbing the ladder of my professional career, the message was always the same: don't show weakness, don't break down. I didn't have the space to cry, to express my pain or fear. The expectation was simple—"man up" and get through it.

In my mind, doing anything else meant admitting defeat, and I refused to let that happen. It was ingrained in me that strength meant enduring, no matter what life threw my way. So I pushed down my emotions, buried my struggles, and kept moving forward—never stopping to address the toll it was taking on me. For years, I believed that was the only way to survive, that showing any form of vulnerability would somehow make me less capable, less strong.

But as time passed, I began to realize that the very things I had been taught to suppress were the very things I needed to face. The strength I thought I was demonstrating wasn't true strength at all—it was simply survival.

Through our time together, Alicia challenged me in this area, and when I entered her office a few days after that horrific night in my apartment, I allowed my dam to break. Before I could really sit down in her comfortable office, I began to sob and release all that had occurred. I felt safe in Alicia's office, and I just couldn't hold it in anymore. Even though my nights had been filled with my tears, as I recalled the events to Alicia, I couldn't stop the flow. I couldn't be strong in the same way I had been thinking about strength. I needed to release, and I could not speak about the nightmare without a flood of tears.

I shared how I was in disbelief that this had occurred. I shared how my faith could not accept what my pastor had said—that God had actually protected me. I was reeling from wondering what I had done to make God *not* protect me. Was God trying to get my attention or something?

I stayed in this place for quite a while. I poured out my questions and my concerns. I wrestled heavily with the why. And Alicia allowed me to stay right there in that space, often just letting me talk and asking me one or two questions along the way. For a very long time, I only asked what I had done wrong to bring about this tragedy. And I'm so very thankful to Alicia for giving me the time and space to do this.

Through a slow evolution of conversations—and occurrences—I eventually was able to get some clarity. And as I'll share in the next chapter, I remember the very moment when it happened—or when I caught up to what God actually did that night.

What messages about therapy have you received from your community? If you haven't received therapy to deal with your trauma, what are some of the issues preventing you from seeking help? Describe your ideal therapist and what you would need from them. How can you, through your actions, serve as an advocate for mental health within your circle?

Advice from a Therapist

Alicia Troff-Meade, LCSW, shares her thoughts on finding the therapist who is best for you.

It's always a good idea to be an informed consumer when it comes to your mental health, so I believe in doing your homework before seeing a therapist.

- Think about what type of therapy is best for your situation: individual, couples, or family therapy.
- Think about what therapy approach would be best for you and your type of problem. There are so many approaches: psychodynamic, behavioral, CBT (cognitive behavioral therapy), DBT (dialectal behavioral therapy), IFS (internal family systems), EMDR (eye movement desensitization reprocessing), ACT (acceptance and commitment therapy). And although this may sound daunting, you can get a quick reference on each one through the Internet.
- Reflect on the professional experience of the therapist, and the personality and style of the therapist that would fit best with yours. Do you like someone who is direct with you or who sits back and listens a lot? Do you work best with someone who is serious or more lighthearted with you? What about someone who is energetic versus phlegmatic and languid? Many people may not think of this as important, but I've found the best success in therapy occurs because the "right fit" between therapist and client has been made.
- Have an idea of what your goal is. What do you want to achieve? What is your purpose? (And hopefully it

isn't about changing someone else, because that will never happen.)

- Have some questions for the therapist to initially answer: What is their philosophy? At the end of the first session, what do they see as your main conflict or struggle? It is definitely OK to ask this question. The therapist probably won't give you a long and detailed answer, but you want to make sure your therapist has listened well and processed in a way that helps you feel understood.

3

BREONNA TAYLOR: TRIGGERS, GRIEF, AND HEALING

WHETHER WE WANT to or not, we probably all recall what we were doing during March 2020. I definitely do. I had just returned home from what was supposed to be my dream trip to Paris. For as long as I can recall, I had wanted to visit Paris, and for the last three years, I had been planning a trip to celebrate my fiftieth birthday. I finally made it.

But my trip was clouded by what had occurred in my life a mere year earlier. Not many people knew the details of that night in February 2019. I had stuffed down the gory details and pushed myself to get back to work, which, as I shared in the previous chapter, ultimately resulted in my not being able to pull it together quickly enough to keep that job. I was struggling. But life went on for everything and everyone around me.

I had to figure out how to move forward despite those forty life-changing minutes that ransacked my apartment and my life. My attorney had been working on my case, but things were moving very slowly as they tend to do when seeking justice, especially in these types of cases. And thank God, my trusted therapist had helped me process a great deal. But an incident like that night isn't wiped away or forgotten (or even recovered from) in a year. I journeyed to Paris anyhow, but my joy and soul had not recovered. The memory of what happened to me was a constant companion, dimming even the lights in the City of Lights. Like everything after that raid, things were not as bright nor as meaningful to me. I walked through life pretty much numb, feeling very little joy, with deep sadness a constant companion. But I pressed on and pushed through. What else could I do?

My travel companion to Paris was Adonica, a dear friend from my church. As we navigated through Charles de Gaulle Airport, ending our seven-day trip, she and I heard rumors of a shutdown because of very contagious virus spreading around the world. Though we didn't know it then, we made it back to Chicago just in time. After I got home to my apartment, I heard some of the same talk I had heard in Paris about a terrible virus circulating. Much was unclear, but airports around the world were shutting down. Companies were sending workers home with orders to work remotely for the foreseeable future. We were in the middle of a pandemic. COVID-19 was spreading rapidly, and nobody was sure how to stop the spread. Thankfully, I was safe in my home with my memories of Paris, trying to get back to my routine even though the pandemic paused everything. It had been a full year since my safe haven of an apartment had been turned into a target that Chicago police officers pounced on as I tried to get dressed for bed. I had been fired from a job, gotten another job, and tried to bury my vacillating emotions as I did the best I could to live my life.

My attorney had filed a lawsuit against the City of Chicago. We had demanded the video recordings from the officers' body cams to show us what happened that night, but the city refused our request, saying it was an ongoing investigation. But we kept fighting. Unfortunately, with the pandemic shutdown, things were not progressing. My case and the gathering of any more information about that night came to a screeching halt, along with the rest of the world.

During the first weeks of the pandemic I was glued to the news, trying to figure out what was going on. One day in March 2020, while I was expecting to hear more about the latest discoveries about this pathogen spreading like wildfire, I heard an interruption to the news. I believe the newscaster said it was breaking news from Louisville, Kentucky. Then they showed a picture of a pretty brown girl dressed in a blue short-sleeved uniform; she looked to be no older than twenty-five. They were reporting that she had been shot dead in her home.

I sat up to pay more attention to the news. The story contrasted with the white noise I had grown used to hearing about the pandemic. After listening to the story out of Louisville for a few more minutes, I realized my body was numb and it was hard to regulate my breathing. I was completely overwhelmed with emotion. For so long, I had struggled to make sense of the night of my raid. *How could the police get it so wrong? How was it possible for them to violate my home, my dignity, and my sense of safety with such recklessness?* No matter how many times I replayed it in my mind, I couldn't find any justification. The injustice of it all weighed on me—the sheer negligence, the lack of accountability. It was a nightmare I couldn't wake up from, a painful reminder of how easily lives can be shattered by those sworn to protect and serve.

As I sat watching the coverage of Breonna Taylor's story unfold, it was impossible to hold back the flood of emotions. The pain hit me like a wave—raw, heavy, and undeniable.

Seeing the police cars swarming outside her home, hearing about how officers lied to her mother about what had happened, and then watching as they arrested her boyfriend as if he were the criminal—it was gut-wrenching. It was like watching my own nightmare play out all over again, except this time, it ended in the worst possible way. Breonna didn't get to wake up the next morning and try to piece her life back together. She didn't get the chance to fight for justice.

The weight of it all was too much to bear. Again I wrestled with how easily law enforcement could shatter someone's life, how effortlessly they could distort the truth to protect themselves, leaving families with nothing but grief and unanswered questions. It was too hard to imagine, yet I didn't have to imagine it—I had lived it. This happened to me. Police had broken into my place too. Like Breonna Taylor, I'd been startled by a break-in in my home; we were not violated by robbers in ski masks but by officers of the law dressed in tactical uniforms. I had my dignity and sanity stolen by police officers. But Breonna—this woman had her life robbed by men in blue.

I could not fully comprehend this story nor what I was feeling, but I couldn't stop soaking up every detail the media shared about her story. Every time it came on the news, I stopped whatever I was doing to listen. I don't know if I needed more information or more details, but there was something about Breonna's story that captivated me. Not many people knew what happened to me a year ago, and through her story, I was reliving the events of the previous year. It felt like déjà vu, but not really. And I was trapped inside my house with my thoughts, my memories, and the news coverage of this young sister who was no longer alive.

I needed to talk to my therapist. Because of the pandemic, I wasn't able to visit Alicia in her office the following Tuesday, so we met via Zoom. As we began our session, she asked her usual questions: "What's going on today? What do you want to talk about?"

I was quick to share: "Did you see the story of the young lady in Kentucky?" I told her that I couldn't stop watching the coverage about Breonna Taylor. I was following the coverage incessantly. And, suddenly, something clicked for me. *This woman lost her life, and I didn't lose mine.* My story could have been much different. My life could have been taken because of a police officer's mistake. The enormity of it hit me: I hadn't died in the raid on my home, but Breonna had. Somehow, God had protected me that night. While I wrestled with where God was and how God could let this happen to me, I got a clear revelation: God *had* been with me and God *had* protected my life that very night. When I was looking for God, He was right there.

While I couldn't understand it, hearing what ended Breonna's life gave me a moment of pause. A flood of emotions continued to surge through my body. I wasn't happy; I couldn't be. This was traumatic. I was shocked, stunned, and forced to relive those moments over and over again while also grieving the life of a young woman I'd never met. I was also grieving my situation all over again. I was stuck and couldn't seem to think of anything else.

Alicia sat with me on Zoom as I processed my emotions. This felt crazy. This felt strange and tough and unbelievable. But in the midst of it all, I finally recognized what my pastor had said: God had protected me. Prior to constantly rewatching Breonna Taylor's story unravel, I hadn't been able to grasp that God had protected me. My place didn't seem protected, and I honestly didn't feel God's hand in the situation. I was still numb and stuck on wondering what I had done to make God take His hand of protection off me. But Breonna's story helped me realize what Pastor Charlie meant when he thanked God for protecting me. I finally got it: God had spared my life. God had indeed protected me the night my world was ransacked.

This breakthrough is another reason I recommend therapy, especially for those who are processing trauma. Alicia helped me own my feelings. I had so much confusion and emotion reeling inside me that I had not fully processed everything related to that night. She helped me put things in perspective as they swam around in my mind and body. She helped me realize that I was grieving my experience by rewatching the Breonna Taylor coverage. Just talking to her prompted the thoughts and emotions I had tried to stuff down below the surface. I thankfully felt comfortable with Alicia and shared with her what I was thinking and feeling and doing—even when I wasn't clear why. Processing these emotions and thoughts with Alicia led to clarity; it led to a breakthrough I had no idea was possible. Alicia surmised that I was grieving not only the story of Breonna Taylor but also the experience. I didn't know her; but I knew her experience, or at least some of it. I was grieving what occurred. I was grieving that we live in a world where this can happen.

Therapist and author of *Her Rites: A Sacred Journey for the Mind, Body, and Soul* Christy Angelle Bauman, PhD, reminds anyone really trying to heal that "there is a ton of grief that has to be had and experienced before we move [on to healing]; you have to grieve what has died in that moment, the innocence of life . . . unfortunately, we don't live in a utopia. We live in a dystopia and that must be grieved even as we continue to live in that place and stay alive and try to thrive. It's a ton of internal work."

During my breakthrough around my commonality with Breonna Taylor, I was flooded with even more feelings. This breakthrough helped to recenter my faith and my thoughts. I hadn't lost faith in God; I always believed in God and that God was all-powerful. This was actually a part of my confusion. I just didn't understand why God didn't intervene and stop these men from raiding my apartment. But, at last, I was able to see God's work during that night.

One way I believe Alicia helped me get to this realization was her acceptance of my feelings and her encouraging me to accept those feelings myself, whatever they were and however confusing they may have felt. She said whatever I was feeling was OK, and it was OK to feel that way.

As humans, we expect certain things and to feel certain ways. Taking the pressure off ourselves to do something in a certain way can bring about liberation; it can free us up to find clarity and perspective. Alicia helped me understand that even when I was angry with God, those feelings were OK. They were valid because they were a part of my story. They were how I felt.

And even in my anger, I don't think I sinned. That may sound strange if you're not religious, but Scripture says, "In your anger do not sin" (Ephesians 4:26). I believe that is a warning against allowing your anger to turn into the action of sinning—allowing it to make you someone you do not want to be. Having a certain feeling or emotion doesn't constitute sin, to me. Acting on it, turning my back on God because I was angry, would have been sinning. No, I kept going to church, kept trying to understand God. My anger was there, but so was my faith. And now, I had more clarity.

No Timeline for Healing

Healing is a process without a true timeline. Camille Quinn from the University of Michigan's School of Social Work says the work associated with healing from trauma is indeed important but very slow, complicated, and to some degree unexplored. Quinn says that she discovered just how much people, particularly the population of Black women, had endured and buried trauma through her work with a substance abuse program. Yes, they were focused on substance abuse and recovery from it, but these women had so many other issues that their traumatic experiences just spilled out of their mouths and bodies—sometimes without them even noticing. They easily said what happened to their grandmother, their mom, or others: domestic violence, rape, neighborhood trauma (like I experienced) was a part of their lives. Quinn found there really wasn't a cultural component to what was already written and being studied. She realized that some of the trauma women were experiencing was familial, but some was also structural and environmentally based.

"We had been normalizing harm," she tells me. And much of the harm women had no control over—like the fear of police. Quinn said she didn't know how some women were even walking around with all the trauma they had buried inside of them and learned to normalize as a part of life. She has dedicated her work to figuring out how people heal and has discovered it is not done in a vacuum. She is dedicated to helping women normalize healing, to make it what we seek and what we crave even when we don't realize the trauma that has been done to us.

"We have to let people know the process of healing is possible. You can heal. Maybe it looks different from someone else's healing, but it is possible. . . . You need to re-create a lifestyle that fortifies a healing process that is for you. By doing this you can regain a sense of agency in your life. You have some control over your life and what is and what is not happening to you.

"The past harms won't go away . . . but when you are healing, as other things crop up that may be traumatic, you have focused on how you heal; you've developed a level of capacity to self soothe and you're not going to let this wreck your spirit today." And the end of the day, she asserts, "We can normalize healing as opposed to harm."

Handling Triggers

The Breonna Taylor footage and story triggered me. In seeing her story, I was reminded of my story. In fact, every news story involving a police raid can trigger me and take me back to February 21, 2019. I know this, and I'm learning how to deal with my triggers. I also realize that triggers—which Dr. Hillary L. McBride defines as "your nervous system remembering something in the past based on something in the present"—are not always bad, nor are they the same. My triggers led to a breakthrough when I processed why I couldn't stop consuming coverage of Breonna Taylor's murder. Speaking with my therapist helped me identify what was going on and shifted my view of God's presence in my life that night when my apartment was raided.

I've learned that you can have not only conscious triggers but also subconscious triggers—not even realizing your body is reacting to a sound, a person, a news story, a smell, etc. After the raid, fireworks became a subconscious trigger for me. I had loved fireworks prior to the raid. I used to go downtown or to Navy Pier on the beautiful Chicago lakefront to enjoy a night out looking at the dazzling colors explode in the sky. Fireworks had been a source of joy, wonder, and celebration—free and fun entertainment. But this beautiful and enjoyable activity turned into a terrible reminder of a night I lost control in my own home.

For me, conscious triggers go off when I'm near a police officer or I see a police car. Things have improved as time has gone on, but this has not always been the case. One night has turned into a lifetime of concerns and issues. One Sunday morning on my way to church, I was pulled over by the police. I hadn't stopped completely at a stop sign, something that might be considered a minor mistake. Any other person might receive a slap on the wrist for this and keep going. But I didn't. I somehow was able to give the officer my license and insurance information. When he went to his car to run my information, I quickly called my pastor in hysteria. I tearfully managed to let him know I had been stopped. He tried to calm me.

When the officer returned to my car, he simply said, "Ms. Young, make sure you come to a complete stop at stop signs." If this happened to someone else, they would have been able to go on with their day and remember to stop at stop signs. I needed my pastor to talk with me and calm me down just so I could continue on my drive.

Another experience that shook me to my core happened while I was trying to enjoy a night out in Chicago. It was a Thursday night. I had gone to an after-work event in the Fulton Market area, a relatively popular neighborhood just blocks from where the wrongful raid on my home happened. I parked in a paid lot, thinking I was making a safe choice. But when I returned to my truck, my stomach dropped—the back window was shattered, and my work bag, along with my work laptop, was gone.

On the surface, having my car broken into wasn't really that big of a deal. It can happen, especially to people living in a large metropolitan area. It is definitely a frustrating and sometimes costly inconvenience. But to a person not living with the type of trauma I have, the next step is as simple as calling the police and your insurance company and perhaps a car windshield company to make the repairs to your car. But what is a minor inconvenience for many people turned into a triggering episode for me. This inconvenience became a crisis. It became a moment of complete emotional collapse, one that sent me spiraling into a breakdown that required therapeutic intervention.

I rushed to find the parking attendant, still trying to process what had happened. His response was casual, almost dismissive, as he was probably very used to this type of incident and patrons' reactions. He said, "I'm really sorry, but we've had a lot of these lately. Just call the police and make a report before you leave."

Just call the police.

What this parking lot attendant didn't understand—what he couldn't understand—was what those words did to me. *Call the police.* Three simple words. To the ordinary person, just a simple step. Pick up the phone, dial 911 or 311, and get the police; an officer in the area would come by, file the report, give me a copy, and send me on my way to deal with my insurance company. But the first step was to call the police. The attendant doling out "simple advice" didn't know my story. He didn't know that less than two miles away, the police he wanted me to call had broken down my door, stormed into my home with guns drawn, and treated me like a criminal. He didn't know that my body still carried the weight of that trauma. He said it so matter-of-factly: call the police.

I walked back to my truck, heart pounding, mind racing. This inconvenience was evolving into a full-blown panic attack. The car break-in triggered a myriad of emotions that I could not control. The parking attendant didn't understand; I couldn't just call the police. I just couldn't.

Instead, I fumbled for my phone, desperate to hear a familiar voice. I don't even remember who I was trying to call, but I know it wasn't the police. I just remember dialing number after number, and with every unanswered call, my panic grew. My heart pounded faster, my hands shook, and my breath became shallow. By the time Keenan, my attorney, finally answered, I was crying uncontrollably, barely able to speak, trying to explain what had happened. I thought to myself, *Who needs to call their attorney from a parking lot after hours when they have a broken car window? Who cries uncontrollably because of a break-in to their car?* This was clearly not just about the break-in.

I wasn't crying because of the broken window or stolen laptop—I was crying because I felt completely unsafe and unprotected once again. I felt like a small inconvenience had turned into a major problem. Because even the thought of calling the police, just blocks from where they violated me, completely shattered me all over again.

Keenan stayed on the phone with me as I somehow managed to drive home. He didn't let me hang up until I was safely parked in my garage. I was again thankful to have such a great relationship with my attorney, who happened to be a deacon at my church and a part of my supportive care team. He always went above and beyond to take care of me. I thanked Keenan and told him I wasn't going to call the police. I'd just get the window fixed and move on.

But I wasn't OK.

I texted Alicia, my therapist, pleading for help. And, as always, she answered. She helped me calm down, regulate my emotions, and remind myself that I was safe in that moment. But I still couldn't sleep that night.

The next morning, I called off work. When I told my supervisor what had happened, she was understanding, but she told me something I had been dreading: "You'll need to go to the police to report the stolen laptop."

Even then, I still couldn't do it.

Keenan, once again, helped me navigate more than my fight against the city—he reminded me that I could file the report over the phone, so I wouldn't have to face any officers in person. Even that small accommodation made the difference between being able to function and falling apart completely. I was able to make that report over the phone rather than go to a police station.

I breathed a sigh of relief once I made the call. One call. It was exhausting to go through all those emotions over a broken car window and a stolen work laptop after trying to have a fun, carefree night out in the city.

This is what trauma looks like. This is what living with PTSD does to you. The smallest, most routine incident can set off emotions you didn't even know you were still carrying. A seemingly simple issue could send me down a path that literally scares me and also takes all my energy—and it can creep up on me in the most unlikely moments.

People assume that when something like a wrongful police raid happens, the worst part is the moment itself—the night they storm in, the humiliation, the terror. But that's not true. The worst part is what happens after. The unpredictable triggers. The moments when you think you're OK, and then suddenly, you're not. You can't even call the police. You live in constant fear that, at any moment, something will happen that will rip the wound wide open again, leaving your emotions raw and unyielding. It's a tough place to live. It's a tough existence, but through healing and therapy, I'm slowly learning to handle some of those triggers.

I'm learning that I have to be intentional with handling any triggers when dealing with the police. I need the tools I've discussed with my therapist to help me coach myself through those times when I'm triggered. This is the case for most people who have experienced trauma. It's not a good feeling to always have to do this, but it is necessary to get through routine parts of life. I've gone through scenarios of what I'd do if I was stopped by the police; what I'd do if police knocked at my door; what I'd do if I encountered an officer. When I know I will be out and about and around police for security reasons, I have to prepare myself. I have to walk through scenarios and repeat mantras to calm myself.

Natasha Smith, in *Black Woman Grief: A Guide to Hope and Wholeness*, quotes Bessel van der Kolk (*The Body Keeps the Score*) for help with dealing with the "imprints" and triggers of trauma on the body, mind, and emotions.

> The challenge of recovery is to reestablish ownership of your body and our mind—of yourself. This means feeling free to know what you know and to feel what you feel without becoming overwhelmed, enraged, ashamed, or collapsed. For most people, this involves:
>
> 1. Finding a way to become calm and focused.
> 2. Learning to maintain the calm in response to images, thoughts, sounds, or physical sensations that remind you of the past.
> 3. Finding a way to be fully alive in the present and engaged with the people around you.
> 4. Not having to keep secrets from yourself including secrets about the ways you managed to survive.

When I realized that watching the Breonna Taylor coverage was a triggering moment, I relied on my therapist Alicia. She helped me recall what she did when I had the major breakthrough of connecting what happened to Breonna Taylor to my raid. It was an aha moment that didn't feel good. I was fixated on the media coverage of this horrific event where the Louisville, Kentucky, police broke into the twenty-five-year-old emergency medical technician's apartment using a no-knock warrant. I relived my nightmare and connected the dots. I had not died, but I certainly could have. Although I did not lose my life that night, I lost so much. When I had this revelation,

I started to hyperventilate and cry. Alicia says she talked with me carefully about the incident. Here are few steps she recalls taking me through:

- Alicia noticed my tension and told me I was in the middle of a flashback; this helped me gain perspective on what was happening, especially in my body.
- Alicia then guided me in breathwork exercises; she helped me slow down my breathing and helped me focus on my inhaling and exhaling. This brought some calmness as I focused on taking in breaths. Sometimes we can forget to breathe in the midst of anxiety and overwhelming feelings; just getting back to deep and intentional breathing helps ground us and calm our nervous system.
- After my breathing was more regulated, Alicia then did a grounding technique: She asked me to name what I saw in the moment. She told me to listen and name the sounds I heard. She also asked me to utilize my sense of smell and observe the odors. These activities helped me refocus and brought me to the present moment. These are exercises I still intentionally practice when I feel overwhelmed or I am triggered.
- After this exercise, Alicia asked me how I was feeling. I was so grateful that she continued to remind me that I was in a safe and secure place. She gave me the freedom to just release my thoughts.
- As a final step, my therapist encouraged me to seek the company of my closest friends, especially when Breonna's case was in the news, and to spend time with my dog, whom she knew was a great emotional support for me.

Breathwork is becoming more and more common in mental wellness practices. According to the Cleveland Clinic, breathwork is "breathing techniques that intentionally channel and focus on the breath." Different breathing techniques are used to calm the body and mind. Practicing breathwork can move the body out of the fight-or-flight mode.

Camille Quinn discusses the benefits of breathing techniques such as the 4-7-8 method. You inhale for four counts, then hold that breath for seven counts, and then exhale for eight counts. Focusing on counting, inhaling, holding your breath, and exhaling slows you down and can calm the mind and reduce anxiety. Simply remembering to breathe or taking a few moments to focus can be a tremendous help when handling anxiety, stress, or post-traumatic triggers. There are also several apps that can keep the time for you when breathing or that offer small circular prompts to assist in calming you down and reminding you to focus on inhaling and exhaling deeply. The Cleveland Clinic website offers several different types of breathing exercises you can try. (See the resources section at the end of this book.)

Utilizing the techniques suggested by your therapist will always be beneficial, but incorporating personalized healing methods tailored to your unique needs can be just as powerful. As we've noted, healing is not a one-size-fits-all journey; it is deeply personal and evolves with self-discovery. What brings you comfort? What environments or activities help you feel grounded and at peace?

I discovered that being near water provided me with a profound sense of tranquility and restoration. There is something incredibly soothing about its presence, whether in motion or at rest. Living in Chicago, I found solace at the lakefront of Lake Michigan—a space that became my personal retreat. The rhythmic crashing of waves against the shoreline serves as a reminder of resilience, demonstrating how even the most forceful tides eventually recede, making way for stillness. On calmer days, the water's glassy surface reflects a peaceful serenity, mirroring the quiet moments of healing I crave. Regardless of its state, water became a metaphor for my own emotional journey—sometimes tumultuous, sometimes serene, but always flowing forward.

In addition to seeking comfort in nature, I also practiced sensory-grounding techniques to stay present and connected to my surroundings. During difficult moments, I would visit a park and intentionally engage my senses. I would take a deep breath and focus on the subtle details around me—the crisp scent of fresh-cut grass, the soft rustling of leaves in the wind, the warmth of the sun against my skin. I paid attention to the texture of my clothing, the weight of my body as I sat on a bench, and the feeling of the earth beneath my feet. This practice helped me shift my attention away from overwhelming thoughts and back into the present moment, anchoring me in reality rather than letting me get lost in stress or anxiety.

Personalized healing techniques allow for deeper engagement and meaningful connection to the process of self-care. While professional guidance provides valuable structure, incorporating elements that resonate with you personally enhances the effectiveness of your healing journey. Whether it's immersing yourself in nature, listening to music, painting, writing, practicing mindfulness exercises, or any number of other things, exploring what truly soothes your mind and body is key.

Healing is a continuous process of exploration and self-awareness. It requires patience, openness, and a willingness to experiment with different techniques until you find what genuinely works for you. For me, water and sensory grounding became essential tools, but for you, it may be something entirely different. The important thing is to allow yourself the space to explore, adapt, and embrace the methods that bring you comfort and peace.

Knowing how to handle your triggers can be helpful when dealing with trauma recovery. Practice can make perfect, so choose a method that works for you and practice it, practice it, practice it. It really is the only way it will become a natural go-to for calming down when you are triggered. The incident that gave you trauma will not be erased, but you can take back your body and emotions and respond to those triggers in a manner that is healthier for you—a manner that allows you to live the life you'd like to live, regardless of what happened to you.

What triggers have you noticed that create intense reactions? How might you uncover the causes of those feelings to promote your healing? What tools can you keep in your toolbox to help you deal with the arresting impact of your triggers?

Advice from a Therapist

Alicia Troff-Meade, LCSW, shares her thoughts on handling triggers associated with trauma.

Triggers, as explained earlier, are experiences from events or situations that have happened in the past but have now moved forward into the present and are causing an emotional reaction in you.

The best way to take care of yourself when you are triggered is to be aware of this. Try to stay as mindful of the present moment as you can, but if you find yourself reacting or being triggered, take the other person out of the situation for a brief moment. Pay attention to your own inner and outer responses (your thoughts, your emotions, your behaviors at the time). Perhaps say to yourself, *This is now, but something has triggered me from the past. Therefore, this is about me and not them.*

Remember that no one *causes* your feelings. Your perceptions create your feelings, and your perceptions involve prior experiences, thoughts, and beliefs. Perceptions are like little cameras that project out into our environment. And like real cameras, there are many filters. It is your choice what filter you want to attach to your camera.

If you are someone who is prone to being triggered, it is important to not see yourself as a victim. How you choose to feel, act, and think is always present. Remind yourself that perception is changeable, because it is your perception. And like one of those pictures that show an old lady or a princess based on what a person is focusing on, try to shift your emphasis to see another side.

Finally, it is wise to practice relaxation and calming techniques. Practice as much as possible these techniques or skills (yoga, somatic bodywork for the vagus nerve, or breathing techniques) even when you're not triggered so that you become proficient and can easily perform them when you need to.

4

A SEARCH FOR ANSWERS

WHEN YOUR WORLD has been upturned by trauma, sometimes it feels as if finding the answers to your many questions might help you heal. You want to know why and how this happened.

After the wrong raid on my sanctuary of a home and life, I searched for answers not only from God but also from the City of Chicago. I thought finding out what happened could help with my healing journey. Maybe if I had more pieces to complete this puzzle, I could get some relief. *Why had the police come to my home? Who was the person on the search warrant whom I had never heard of? What kind of surveillance, if any, had been done to show that this person was connected with the place I had lived in for almost five years?* I needed some answers—something to go on and make this make sense.

During my search for answers, I also gained a heightened sensitivity to and awareness of other incidents involving police in the wrong place and wrongly damaging lives forever. Whenever I saw a news story involving suspicious activity by the police, I stopped and paid special attention. I later pulled up any stories I could find and read them like a ferocious reporter looking for a lead. I became my own detective, sniffing out clues and repeatedly reviewing any documents I could obtain. I just wanted some insight into what would make twelve officers break in and take over my apartment. Every time I uncovered a possibility, I stopped. *Could this be why these twelve men converged on my home? Could this be why God left me unprotected at this time? Why? Why? Why?* During every free moment, my mind was flooded with these questions—and they often crept into my mind when I wasn't free. Living like this is exhausting. Looking for answers that don't really help you is no way to heal, but I just couldn't stop.

Although watching the Breonna Taylor case unfold shed light on how differently my situation could have turned out and helped me reshape my thoughts around God's protection of me that night, I still had many, many questions. Collecting information became critical to me. I sought answers and I sought justice. I probably drove my attorney crazy as I presented my case to him and adamantly declared that I wanted all twelve of those officers fired! How dare they walk around vowing to "serve and protect" citizens, yet somehow they ransacked my life and apartment! My sorrow and disappointment had a constant companion of anger. I needed to find out what was going on and make each police officer who invaded my apartment that night pay. I wasn't going to stop until I got some justice and some answers.

I was prepared to do battle no matter how long it took.

In addition to reading and watching all news stories remotely related to the police and wrongful use of power or force, I read any and everything on the law. What were officers required to do? What were citizens' rights? I found out pretty early that I was supposed to receive a copy of the search warrant as soon as the officers entered my home; the body cam footage shows me asking to see the warrant multiple times, but I wasn't given the paper until the very end of the botched raid, after all the damage had been done—both physically and psychologically.

My attorney Keenan, who specializes in civil rights and personal injury, shared that when he watched this part of the video it immediately reminded him of the movie *Training Day* with Denzel Washington. In this movie, Washington played a corrupt officer who waved a piece of paper, pretending it was a valid search warrant, when in reality it was nothing of the sort. The scene had always stuck with me, but now I was living my own version of that moment. The difference? In my case, the warrant was real—but the way it was handled was just as deceptive, just as infuriating. Instead of being presented with the warrant before the chaos unfolded, I was handed it after the officers had already ransacked my home. It wasn't a formal procedure; it was an afterthought. A half-hearted attempt at protocol, given to me as they were leaving, as if that single piece of paper justified everything they had just put me through. One of the officers muttered a vague, insincere apology—one that didn't even begin to scratch the surface of the humiliation, fear, and rage boiling inside me.

The night of the raid, I sat there gripping the document with trembling hands, my mind spinning. *Why now? Why after the fact?* The anger in my chest burned hotter with each passing second. This wasn't justice. This wasn't how things were supposed to happen. I should have been given the warrant before my home was stormed. I should have been treated with dignity. Instead, I was left standing in the wreckage of my own living room, forced to piece together the legal justification for my own violation.

I read the papers, my eyes scanning the words, but all I could see was red. This wasn't just about a warrant—it was about the way they wielded their power, and the damage they left in their wake. They said the warrant was to search my address for a person whose name I had never heard before.

I was baffled. I had no idea who the person was whose name was on the search warrant; he certainly didn't live in my home. I had lived in this apartment since 2015. I had never even received a piece of mail with his name on it, so I was certain he hadn't ever walked through the doors of my home. I doubt he was ever even connected to my address.

Award-winning local reporter Dave Savini of CBS Chicago and his team found out pretty early on that the police had filed this search warrant based on a tip from an informant. Savini says that with just a little bit of digging he found the man whose name was on the search warrant, and he had nothing to do with me or my apartment. Savini recalls, "My team of producers started running background checks on the target and found he was released from jail with an electronic monitoring bracelet. He was a man with some priors who had lived in her neighborhood and also in one of the units next to [Anjanette's] apartment."

Now this bit of information makes me shake my head. It leads to more confusion than clarity. I can't figure out why police officers wouldn't know where this young man was, because he wore an electronic monitor. They had not done enough research, and they had not communicated with other law enforcement departments. This whole thing could have been fixed with just a bit of care and due diligence, in my opinion. I didn't have to go through this nightmare.

But I also wasn't the first. Dave also says he and his team "had already established a database from two prior years of exposing wrong raids and knew the Chicago Police Department was overwhelmingly executing search warrants in Black and Brown communities."

Was the due diligence bypassed because of the color of my skin? How could things have gone so utterly wrong? How could they break down my door and search my apartment based on information that had no connection with me? Was it really about race?

As I began the legal process—first demanding the city take action against the officers and then filing a lawsuit when they would not agree to any of my terms—my great lawyer tried to set expectations of what would happen. After hearing me repeatedly say I wanted the officers fired, he calmly explained, "Anjanette, it doesn't work that way." He advised me to take steps to get the city to cooperate and make systematic changes to protect others. We began by sending a letter of demand requesting restitution but, more important, punishment of the officers. We asked for a much smaller amount of money than I later received. I didn't want money, really. I wanted justice. I wanted reform. I wanted the police to do their job and thoroughly research whose house they were breaking into before they disrupted another life on an anonymous tip.

The city responded to our initial demand letter—again, what we were asking for financially wasn't even half of what they ended up settling for—by saying, "Our officers did nothing wrong . . . this is a zero-dollar case." Their response was literally that nothing had been done wrong. Nothing. And they made no promises of reform or even punishment for the officers involved.

I simply could not wrap my mind around the city's response. How could these men not be held accountable for what they did to me, to my life, and to my home? The sheer injustice of it all was unbearable. I had been violated in the most dehumanizing way, yet the system was treating it as if it were nothing—a mere inconvenience rather than a life-altering event. From the start, my goal in pursuing legal action against the city was never about money. I wanted justice. I wanted accountability. I wanted them fired. I wanted every single officer who participated in that horrific raid to face consequences for their actions. But when I heard that the city's stance was that they had done nothing wrong—that they bore zero responsibility—and that this case would likely result in no financial settlement, I felt my heart shatter.

Tears welled up in my eyes as frustration and disbelief consumed me. I turned to my attorney, my voice breaking as I said, "This doesn't make sense. Every other profession is held accountable. If a doctor makes a mistake and harms a patient, they can be sued, and their malpractice insurance is used to make things right. Even as a social worker, if I harm someone—whether intentionally or unintentionally—I would lose my job. So why do these officers get to destroy my life and walk away without consequences?"

It felt like a cruel joke, one that played on repeat in a system designed to protect power rather than people. The message was clear: My suffering didn't matter. My pain was invisible to those in charge. And worst of all, justice wasn't even a consideration.

The city's response just made my anger intensify and my depression grow deeper. I didn't understand why police were held to a different standard. The accountability group for the Chicago Police Department, the Civilian Office of Police Accountability (COPA), had started an investigation, but we wouldn't hear a word from them until eighteen months after the botched raid. When I pressed for answers as to why, the review board said officers kept canceling their appointments. The overseeing committee couldn't even interview them, and it was a part of their policy to talk with each officer about the events of that night. Because the officers kept canceling their appointments, the review of what happened to me that night was at a standstill. I couldn't even get relief or answers from the board overseeing police accountability.

So for more than a year and a half, I sat in my anger as my attorney and I searched for answers and accountability. I also sat in my sadness, which led me to a deep, deep depression. I only told a few people about what happened, because what would I say? How could I repeat the nightmare that had rocked my world on an ordinary Thursday night?

In the beginning, I kept my story to myself. I barely told anyone what had happened, offering only the most basic explanation to my boss. As I mentioned, I took just one day off before forcing myself to return to work, convincing myself that pushing through was the best way to regain control. But it didn't take long to realize that no matter how much I tried to act as if things were normal, I was not the same person anymore. My entire life had been altered—not because of anything I did, but because of a name on a search warrant, a name that wasn't even mine. A mistake, a failure in due diligence—whatever it was, it didn't matter. What mattered was that I was left to pick up the pieces.

My mind, once sharp and focused, now felt like it was drowning in fog. I struggled to concentrate, to engage, to be the professional I had worked so hard to become. The simplest tasks felt overwhelming. I was physically present at work, but mentally and emotionally, I was somewhere else—trapped in a cycle of disbelief, fear, and exhaustion.

Each day, I went through the motions. I showed up, completed what I could, and made it through. Then I'd return home, take care of Lexi, and try to find some sense of normalcy in the quiet of my apartment. But the silence was never comforting. Instead, it was where my mind unraveled. The nights were the hardest—when the distractions faded, and I was left alone with my thoughts. Most nights, I cried myself to sleep—if sleep ever came. The weight of it all was crushing, and I didn't know how much longer I could keep pretending I was OK.

While I continued to work with Alicia, which helped tremendously, I refused to even entertain her suggestion to begin a medication for my depression. Nope. That's not what I do, I told her. That's not what I had been conditioned to do as a Black woman. I watched my grandmother work hard and push through. I watched women around me take abuse and keep moving. I thought Alicia was coming from a perspective that was counter to who I was as a strong, resilient Black woman.

Yet I suffered. When I was eventually let go from my job around September 2019, I kind of thought of it as a relief. I knew I could find another job. I got a new job soon after at another hospital. But the new job wouldn't erase the memories flooding my mind. The new job wouldn't relieve my desire for answers from the city. My new job didn't solve the problem I knew we had about police reform.

So, like the stereotypical strong Black woman, I kept powering through, or so I thought. I did what I could to get through work and rushed home to do more research. I called Keenan often and asked more and more questions that could not be answered. In 2020, when we were forced to work from home and stop attending outside events, my depression worsened as the isolation from the pandemic overtook the world and me. Yet I still didn't want to succumb to taking medicine. It just wasn't what "we" do.

A few months before the pandemic shut us down and we witnessed news reports about Breonna Taylor, George Floyd, and the mayhem across the country and dissension around police brutality, I saw a local story on my favorite news station, CBS Chicago. The report was part of the two-year investigation reporter Dave Savini and his team had done titled *[un]warranted*. Dave and I weren't yet in touch, but this documentary series put him on my radar. In the first part of the series that I saw, he highlighted police raids and the impact they had on families, who were disproportionately Black and Brown. In some cases, children were in the home, the officers had the wrong address, and suspicious tips were utilized to burst into homes with search warrants. One of the stories in this series reported that between 2016 and 2019 in Chicago, police had raided approximately five thousand homes, all in Black and Brown communities. And none of these raids had led to arrests. Doors were left broken, possessions were overturned, and children were questioned without adults present.

One of the stories in Savini's series highlighted the case of Peter Mendez, a young boy who was only nine years old when Chicago police officers burst into his family's home—because of a "tip" from an informant, which was eerily close to my case. The police officers had guns drawn on everyone in the household, including Peter and his younger brother. As I heard Savini's report, I realized that was my story too. I quickly contacted Keenan and asked him if he thought it was a good idea to tell my story to CBS Chicago. He asked if I wanted to open up and share. I said, "Nothing is happening in court—I may as well try the media." Keenan pressed and asked if I was sure. I replied, "I'm not sure I want to do this, but this is all we have right now."

Keenan wanted me to know that contacting the media would change my story from my personal ordeal to a much more public story. I would be forced to take my grief and pain and anger public, and that's a whole 'nother layer of pushing past trauma. What was once just between me and my attorney and a few friends would become shared with anyone watching the news. My shame and embarrassment would be on full display; but otherwise, I'd have to watch the city get away with holding out on giving us information and not forcing these officers to take any accountability.

No, I didn't want to go public with my story. I felt like the City of Chicago was forcing me to relive and expose the most traumatic moment of my life—not for my own healing, but as a necessary cost of exposing a corrupt system. But the need for accountability outweighed my need for privacy. I hadn't asked to be in this fight, but I was given no choice. If I wanted justice, I had to come forward, to tell my story over and over again, to lay bare my pain in the public eye.

Being forced into the spotlight disrupted my healing. It pulled me away from the quiet, internal work I was trying to do and placed me in a battle that demanded all my energy. It forced me to shift, to fight harder, and to prepare myself for a different kind of struggle—one that required not just emotional resilience but also public courage.

I told Keenan, "I refuse to be a passive victim." I was angry—enraged—and I wanted to fight back with everything in me. I refused to sit back and let this moment define me without a fight. I needed to know everything about my case. I needed to see the paperwork, the reports, the evidence—anything that could help me understand why this had happened to me. I needed answers, and I was determined to find them.

Knowing the facts, searching for the truth—it became part of my healing process. It gave me something to hold on to when everything else felt out of my control. While I didn't get an answer from God right away, I was determined to get an answer from the system. I needed to know why this had happened—because without understanding, how could I ever begin to move forward? My attorney proceeded to reach out to another attorney who knew Dave Savini at CBS Chicago. When this attorney told the reporter about me and my story, Dave requested to be connected with Keenan. Dave says as soon as he heard some of the details, he thought the story was suspicious and should be investigated. He knew from his other research that this was a story to look into. He also thought his team could help Keenan gain the records he needed from the city, including the body cam footage the city was still holding on to and not releasing to us.

When Dave and I spoke, Dave quickly caught on to the devastating impact of my story. Even though he didn't have the body cam footage, he believed me. He recalls, "Anjanette Young's story was compelling and a disgraceful display of police conduct and even though I didn't have the body camera footage yet, I still believed every word she told me." Dave says when he got a copy of the search warrant the police used to break into my place, he immediately realized the police had erred. He was easily able to find the man listed on the warrant. Certainly, the police could have found the same young man rather easily—if they had exercised some care and due diligence.

As Dave looked into my story, he says, his team pretty quickly was able to establish that "the police were failing to follow their own policies and procedures." The Chicago Police Department has a policy stating they are never to take the word of an informant without vetting the information, Dave explains. They are also supposed to first make sure the target is not already incarcerated or in police custody. "We immediately knew this raid should not have occurred at her address, so we knew we had a story even without the body camera footage. We figured the body cams would eventually get released after we told her first story because we called out the city for trying to cover it up." Dave was banking on the fact that Chicago Mayor Lori Lightfoot would feel the pressure to release the video footage, "since she ran for office vowing to stop wrong raids based on our work on the series *[un]warranted* from 2018."

Initially, I felt the same way as Dave about Mayor Lightfoot. She was the first Black female mayor of Chicago, and I was a proud supporter of hers. Dave was right—she ran on the issue of police accountability and had once served as the president of the Chicago Police Board and chair of the Chicago Police Accountability Task Force. I thought that as a Black woman, she'd want to stop this type of discrimination and careless treatment of people in Black and Brown communities. She even came to my church at the beginning of her campaign and outlined what she would do. I believed her, trusted her, and supported her with my vote. The raid on my home didn't even occur under her administration, so again I thought she'd clearly do the right thing and hold the police department accountable. I was sorely disappointed.

Despite Mayor Lori Lightfoot's early assurances of reform, meaningful change within the Chicago Police Department never materialized. When she took office, she presented herself as a leader committed to accountability and justice, giving hope to those demanding an end to the city's history of wrongful raids and police misconduct. Just two days into her term, she assured Dave Savini that she would "make changes." Yet, as time passed, it became painfully clear that her words were just rhetoric. Under her leadership, there was no substantial progress in addressing the systemic failures that allowed these egregious violations to persist.

The urgent need for reform was undeniable. For years, innocent residents had been subjected to wrongful raids—incidents like mine in which heavily armed officers burst into homes, guns drawn, only to discover they had targeted the wrong address. These mistakes left families terrified, humiliated, and in some cases, physically harmed. Victims demanded change. Advocates pushed for stricter policies. However, the much-needed overhaul of the Chicago Police Department's search warrant procedures remained at a standstill, leaving those affected to wonder if justice would ever be served.

By March 2021, frustration had reached a boiling point. Illinois Attorney General Kwame Raoul publicly condemned the lack of action, making it clear that the Lightfoot administration had failed to implement the necessary reforms. In an interview with WTTW, Chicago's public television station,

Raoul expressed deep concern over the ongoing failures of city leadership in addressing the Chicago Police Department's deeply flawed approach to search warrants. He pointed to the continued use of no-knock raids—violent, unannounced police entries that placed innocent lives in danger and disproportionately affected marginalized communities.

Raoul's criticism was not just theoretical; it also reflected the lived experiences of real people—people like me. I know firsthand the terror of a wrongful raid and the trauma that lingers long after, trauma compounded by the knowledge that I was far from alone. Countless others have endured similar injustices, yet city officials failed to take the necessary steps to ensure it would never happen again.

Raoul did not mince words—he called for the Chicago Police Department to ban no-knock search warrants outright or, at the very least, impose strict limitations on their use. His stance underscored a fundamental issue: Despite mounting public outcry and undeniable evidence of harm, city leadership remained stagnant. The administration had ample opportunity to enact meaningful reform, yet the promise of change never evolved beyond empty words.

In the end, the reality was clear—Lightfoot's administration did not deliver the reform it once vowed to implement. For the victims of wrongful raids, justice remained out of reach, and the systemic failures of the Chicago Police Department continued unchecked. The question remains: how many more innocent lives must be disrupted before real change is finally made? My frustration became so great that eventually I actively campaigned against Mayor Lightfoot during her reelection bid in 2023. She had the opportunity to bring about real change but failed to deliver.

When the time came for voters to decide, it was clear that many shared my frustration—she didn't even make it to the runoff. Her leadership had fallen short, and the city needed someone who would truly listen, take action, and be accountable to the people.

During the election, I threw my support behind Brandon Johnson, believing that his vision for Chicago aligned more closely with the urgent reforms our city needed. His promises of change resonated with those of us who had been demanding justice, accountability, and a shift in how the city handles issues like police misconduct and community investment. When he won, it felt like a step in the right direction, but my work didn't stop there.

Supporting a candidate doesn't mean giving them a free pass—it means holding them accountable once they take office. Since Johnson's election, I've made it a point to keep the pressure on, ensuring that his administration follows through on its commitments. While progress has been slow, there are signs that the city is finally listening and beginning to respond. Change is never instantaneous, but what matters is that the movement toward meaningful reform continues.

Chicago's future depends on leaders who don't just make promises but take real, measurable action. I will continue to advocate, push for accountability, and demand results—because our communities deserve nothing less.

But when I first viewed Dave Savini's docuseries, Lightfoot was still mayor, and my hopes were still high that we might see change. After Dave heard my story, he was quick to get to work on the investigation. When he agreed to do my story, he too requested the release of that night's video footage from the body cameras police were legally supposed to wear. FOIA is supposed to allow anyone the freedom to ask for such data. However, Dave's request was denied too. The city said the footage was a part of an ongoing internal investigation.

Because of the roadblock from this denial, Dave's first story on my case got very little attention—that happens when you don't have video to show people. For some reason, our visual senses have taken over and dictate what we tune in to. Without that footage of me screaming in my apartment as twelve men turned over my belongings, many people barely heard the words of the story about a Black woman on the Near West Side of Chicago whose life was upturned by a wrongful raid one night in February 2019. Yet I still had to go through the traumatic events and details again, this time with an audience, even if smaller than desired.

Dave says he knew he had to take on my story and look into it more thoroughly. "We knew Anjanette's case was special because any woman or man could relate to her case; she could be someone's mother, daughter, or sister. She was also someone who wasn't seen as a real person during the raid. We felt she was an extremely strong person who wanted more than a settlement, what she wanted was accountability and sweeping reforms to protect others. She is also a woman of faith, and her church community also played in a role in the pushing part because that community got behind her in full force. If it could happen to her, it could happen to anyone."

Dave, Keenan, and our teams all kept pushing—as much as we could with a pandemic slowing everything down. Nearly two years after the raid, on December 17, 2020, after several rounds of legal challenges—and some very strategic and wise moves by Keenan—we finally received the body cam footage. We had to jump through some hoops, file several petitions, and basically force the city to release the footage of the police raiding my home that night. When we finally received it, Keenan and I gladly turned over the footage to Dave and his team.

Keenan confessed to having trouble viewing the footage. He called me and assured me that it would be handled carefully. He saw my naked body, had even more concern for me, and was more convinced that the city should be held accountable. This was just wrong. Dave allowed only two women on his staff to view the raw footage, knowing that I was naked during a portion of it. These two women worked closely with me about how much should be blurred to honor my privacy and decency.

When CBS Chicago ran a teaser about the story disclosing that never-before-seen body cam footage would be shown, the city tried to stop the station from running the story. The city's lawyers filed an emergency motion before a federal judge to try to stop the story from airing. The city said the footage was privileged and protected by a court order that prohibited us from sharing it with the media.

CBS Chicago pressed forward. Dave says, "We felt if we could convince her attorney to give us the video, the risk of getting sanctioned by the court [was outweighed by] the public's right and Anjanette Young's right to see the truth of what happened."

Dave admits, "It was a bold move by Anjanette Young and Keenan Saulter as the city would eventually threaten them both with sanctions. CBS also made the decision to air the story anyway, even if the judge ruled against us. I guess some things are worth fighting for in this world."

Just minutes before the story was scheduled to air, despite the emergency motion to stop the CBS team, the station won the legal battle. A judge issued his order mere minutes before the live broadcast. He said CBS could air the videos; they had nothing to do with the court orders.

And so, on that Thursday night at 10:00 PM on CBS Chicago, viewers in the city of Chicago and surrounding areas heard my screams and saw my blurred, exposed body. They witnessed the chaos as officers stormed into my home, weapons drawn, their voices commanding me to comply. They heard me pleading—desperately trying to tell them they had the wrong home. What had once been my private nightmare was now public, raw, and impossible to ignore.

The response was immediate and overwhelming. The city erupted. People were outraged, disturbed by what they had just witnessed. The sheer violation, the brutality, the blatant disregard for my dignity—it struck a chord that couldn't be silenced. My story spread like wildfire, and within hours, every major news outlet in Chicago was covering it. The public wanted answers.

As the footage circulated, my phone started ringing nonstop—reporters, activists, supporters all wanting to hear more, to understand the depths of what had happened to me. Requests for interviews flooded in, and my name suddenly became a Twitter hashtag at the center of a conversation I never asked to be part of. My trauma was no longer just mine. It had become a symbol, a case study in injustice, and I was being called to step into a role I wasn't sure I was ready for.

But there was no escaping it now. The world had seen. The world had heard. And the question loomed over me: What now? How do you take something so personal, so painful, and turn it into something bigger? Something that demands justice? Something that refuses to let the system bury yet another victim under the weight of indifference?

Just before the story with the footage aired, I spoke with my boss at the job I had been at for about a year. And thankfully, she handled things differently than the boss I first told about the raid. I asked my boss if she watched the news and alerted her that a story about me was about to run; she admitted she mostly watched news from her native Puerto Rico, so she had not heard about my case. I explained what happened, and she immediately showed care for my well-being. She asked if she could do anything and what I needed from her during this time. I said, "I don't know what I need." She then proceeded to let me know she was going to set up an appointment for me with HR to discuss my options if I needed time to care for myself. My manager treated me with the care and dignity I believe we should share with God's creation, humanity. She brought me to HR, where I was able to learn more about what I could do. Her reaction was a bright spot in this ordeal. She was truly concerned with my well-being.

The broader community often doesn't know what is available to them when dealing with trauma, and they may not have advocates guiding them and ensuring they know their options. Not knowing can hinder the healing process. Having someone who cares enough to help you find the right resources can be life-changing.

I was told I could take a mental health break or a leave of absence. Initially, I didn't take either option, because I felt I could handle things as I was still working remotely during the pandemic. But as my story broke—this time with video footage of my nightmare—I received nonstop requests for interviews, which meant I had to repeat and relive this story far more than I had ever anticipated. I spoke with reporters from the *Chicago Tribune*, *Chicago Sun-Times*, ABC 7, and countless other media outlets, and each interview meant retelling and reliving the most traumatic night of my life. At first, I felt a sense of obligation to share my story, to bring awareness to the injustice I had suffered. But with every interview, I found myself emotionally drained, struggling to balance the fight for justice with my own healing. I realized I needed to focus on fighting this ordeal as well as my healing, and one could not be sacrificed for the other.

So I decided that while it was important to speak out, make others aware of what happened to me, and demand accountability, I also had to protect my own well-being. The weight of continuously revisiting that night was taking a toll on me—mentally, emotionally, and physically. I knew that if I didn't set boundaries, if I didn't allow myself the space to heal, I would be consumed by the very thing I was fighting against. And that is also when I decided to take my HR benefits seriously and take a leave from work. At first, I thought I could pull through this thing, but I just couldn't. I'm glad I had the information about the HR benefits available to me, thanks to my boss's earlier insistence that I speak with HR about possibilities. I went on short-term disability, which later commuted to long-term disability.

My public battle extended the trauma, but I was committed to fighting. Taking the story public meant a different approach to my healing. Every time I speak to a reporter—even to this day—or stand in front of a crowd and share my story, I have to mentally and emotionally prepare myself. I know there will be footage of that night, and I will hear my voice shouting and screaming that they have the wrong place over and over. Just sharing my story reopens the wounds and the pain, so I have to prepare. I normally pray a lot before and after speaking about the raid. I listen to my worship music and get my mind in a space to share. I think about why I'm doing this. It's not to share the gory details and relive this nightmare; it's to let people know what is happening in our communities. It's to open up what has been a closed door on a nasty secret that leaves people hurt and forever scarred. It's to demand that more care and caution are used, even in Black and Brown communities. It's to hold the police's feet to the fire and demand better treatment for God's people. I have to tell myself that over and over to focus and get ready to open up and share more about what happened that night. Though I relive that night each time I share the story, and that's tough, I've determined that it's worth it.

No Medicine for This Black Woman

After going public and reopening up about this story, my therapist saw how much I was suffering. Even after consistent visits with her via Zoom, and some in person, I was still nowhere near the Anjanette I was before this ordeal. Alicia again suggested I consider taking some form of medication to help me. No, I repeated. As a clinician, I had seen the failure of medicine. I knew too many cases of people taking medicine and suffering more from the side effects. I knew the systemic issues around doctors just wanting to throw pills at a problem without taking the time to find the appropriate dose. I understood that took time and money, and I just didn't think I needed medicine. I was going to fight this with God's help. No, I was not going to take medicine.

But after one of my most severe triggering episodes—one that left me completely unraveled and landed me in the emergency room—I was forced to rethink my stance on taking medication. Until that moment, I had resisted medication, convinced that I could push through my trauma on my own. But when the Fourth of July weekend arrived and fireworks exploded in my neighborhood, I realized just how fragile and frayed my nervous system had become. The first loud boom sent a shockwave through my body. My heart pounded, my breathing became erratic, and within seconds I was spiraling. I wasn't hearing fireworks anymore—I was reliving terror. My mind and body betrayed me, collapsing into fear before I even understood what was happening. I slid down to the floor of my bedroom, curling up in a corner, feeling completely disconnected from reality. I couldn't move. I couldn't think. I couldn't pull myself out.

That moment forced me to acknowledge that my body and mind needed help. I could no longer pretend that sheer willpower would be enough. Trauma had rewired me, and I needed more than just strength—I needed healing. And maybe, just maybe, that healing required me to accept something I had been resisting all along: that medication wasn't a sign of weakness, but a tool for survival.

Maybe I couldn't get through this without some outside help. I listened to my primary doctor and Alicia and agreed to start with a very low dosage of medication to help my depression. Alicia let me know that at least this this low dose of medicine might help me get some sleep, and my body needed that part of the healing severely. I'm thankful I had the benefit of providers who listened to me and took my concerns seriously. I had respect and I had help to manage the medicine.

Tammy Lewis Wilborn, PhD, sheds light on the dilemma many Black women face when it comes to taking medication to help with mental health. In her book *Playing a New Game*, she says, “Needing and taking medication does not mean that something is wrong with you or that your worth decreases should you need to take it. Look at medication as another tool in your toolbox to help you be well and flourish.”

She breaks down more reasons people don’t want to take medicine. Perhaps clients are concerned that their issues are not “serious enough” for medicine or perhaps they are concerned about the side effects. She says all these reasons are valid concerns and encourages clients to explore and then think about them. She recommends a thorough evaluation with your counselor or other trusted medical provider. “Taking medication can be a powerful tool in your toolbox for achieving mental and emotional stability.”

Taking medicine isn’t a death sentence. It doesn’t have to be taken for the rest of your life, but just until you feel better and are able to operate more like yourself. I found it hard to sleep, so when I finally did give in to taking medicine, my sleep improved. When my sleep improved, my mental outlook got a little better. Medicine was a building block for me to be able to do other things that could help me heal.

Medication helped, but unfortunately, finding the answers to what really happened that night did not give me relief. I had thought the answers would be another building block on my road to healing, but they didn’t help me. They made me angrier. They came through Dave’s team, our own investigation, and other information that was disseminated through the report from COPA—about eighteen months after the raid.

Through these avenues, I eventually learned that there had been a young man in my neighborhood, the young man whose name appeared on the search warrant the police used to raid my home, who had been picked up for something unrelated to me. The police made a deal with this young man: if he told them the location of someone else they were looking for who supposedly had guns and drugs, the police would let the informant go. The police officers put their informant in a car and drove him down my block. He pointed to my door, the only door painted red in a row of apartments. He told the police, "He lives at the one with the red door." And with that simple piece of information, the cops got my address and proceeded to obtain a warrant to search for the gun of the man who had never stepped foot in my apartment. My red door became an easy target for an informant to single out, and my life would never be the same.

I also discovered that even the way the police obtained the search warrant was deeply flawed and reckless. The judge who signed off on it wasn't even a criminal court judge; he was a traffic judge who just happened to be on call that night. That alone should have raised concerns about the integrity of the warrant, but the carelessness didn't stop there. The officers failed to conduct even the most basic investigative work before storming into my home. They never watched the building to see who actually lived there. They never checked utility bills or rental agreements, or reached out to the leasing office—any one of which would have told them I had absolutely no connection to the person they were looking for. Instead, they relied on the word of a young man facing charges—someone with every reason to say whatever it took to shift the attention off himself. He didn't give them an exact address, a name, or any solid evidence. All he did was point to a red door in a row of green ones. That was all it took for the police to decide they had enough reason to break into my home, guns drawn, ready for a dangerous confrontation.

And so, based on a vague, unreliable tip and zero verification, they arrived at my apartment with a no-knock warrant, looking for a man I had never met—someone who, as it happened, was already wearing an electronic monitor that could have told them exactly where he was. Instead of using common sense, technology, or standard police procedures, they chose force over facts. And in doing so, they shattered my sense of security, my peace, and my faith in the system meant to protect me.

While researching Chicago's complex history, I came across a website titled Chicago Gang History. It uncovered the rich yet troubled history of the community where I lived—a history that I was not aware of when deciding to move there, but one I later come to believe played a role in why and how this raid happened. At the time, my home was in a redeveloped community called Westhaven Park, a mixed-income neighborhood consisting of townhomes and larger apartment buildings. But Westhaven Park had not always existed. Before its transformation, the land was home to one of Chicago's most infamous public housing projects: the Henry Horner Homes. The Henry Horner Homes once spanned ten blocks on the Near West Side of Chicago. These public housing projects were named after Henry Horner, the first Jewish governor of Illinois, who served from 1933 to 1940. Horner was known for his progressive policies and dedication to social welfare during the Great Depression, making it fitting that a housing development intended to provide affordable living for low-income families was named in his honor.

When the Henry Horner Homes were first constructed, they were considered an ideal place to live. Built as part of Chicago's broader public housing initiatives, the complex was initially well maintained, offering working-class families access to stable, affordable housing. However, like many other public housing projects in Chicago, the conditions at Henry Horner deteriorated over time due to a combination of systemic neglect, economic decline, and the rise of gang activity.

By the mid-1980s, Henry Horner had become one of the most dangerous housing complexes in the city. The influx of gangs turned the area into a battleground for drug trafficking and violent crime, making everyday life perilous for residents. As crime surged, the Chicago Police Department developed a contentious relationship with the community. Rather than working to protect and serve the residents, the department often treated everyone who lived there as if they were criminals. Many residents reported that police were slow to respond to emergency calls, and when they did arrive, their treatment of the community was often marked by hostility and disrespect.

By the 1990s, public outcry and federal intervention led to a shift in Chicago's approach to public housing. The city adopted a strategy of demolishing high-rise public housing complexes and replacing them with mixed-income developments in an effort to integrate communities and reduce concentrated poverty. In 2010, the last of the original Henry Horner Homes was demolished, marking the end of an era. In its place, the city constructed new mixed-income housing units, designed to foster a more diverse and stable environment.

While the transformation of Henry Horner into Westhaven Park was framed as a symbol of progress, it carried deep racial and socioeconomic tensions. It still bore the stigma of being associated with poverty, crime, and instability—perceptions that I believe influenced how law enforcement viewed and treated the area. The raid on my home wasn't just a random mistake; it was part of a larger pattern—one in which police targeted certain communities without proper investigation or accountability. If I had lived in a high-rise in the Loop or a luxury building along Lake Shore Drive, would they have burst through my door with a no-knock warrant, guns drawn, without verifying who lived there? Or was it because I lived in a historically Black and Brown and low-income neighborhood that they felt entitled to act first and ask questions later?

Gaining a deeper understanding of my community's history gave me a clearer perspective on the systemic failures that had shaped my experience. My story wasn't just about one night of injustice—it was about decades of neglect, racial biases, and policing disparities that had long dictated how residents in my neighborhood were treated. The injustices I faced were part of a much larger pattern, one that stretched back generations, rooted in policies that marginalized and criminalized entire communities rather than supporting and uplifting them.

When the Henry Horner Homes were demolished as part of Chicago's broader public housing transformation, the city marketed the new mixed-income units as a symbol of progress. These townhomes were advertised as modern, desirable residences on the edge of the rapidly growing West Loop, just a mile away from downtown's attractions. The promise of a fresh start, a safer environment, and access to better resources were what initially drew me to the area. Like many others, I saw potential in this new chapter.

Writer Alex Kotlowitz exposed the devastating conditions of the Henry Horner Homes in his award-winning book, *There Are No Children Here: The Story of Two Boys Growing Up in the Other America*. The book, which painted a harrowing picture of poverty, violence, and systemic neglect, was later adapted into a film. This was the history that still shaped the way the police saw my neighborhood, even after redevelopment. I firmly believe that, in the eyes of some officers, Westhaven Park was still the Henry Horner Homes.

No one deserves to be treated unfairly, regardless of where they live. But when a community has a contentious history with law enforcement, assumptions and biases take over. I became a victim of that kind of careless, prejudiced thinking. The police didn't see me as an individual—a professional woman, a law-abiding citizen, someone who had nothing to do with their suspect. They saw a red door in a neighborhood they still associated with crime. That was enough to justify storming into my home with a no-knock warrant, guns drawn, and no attempt to verify who actually lived there.

Uncovering the history of my neighborhood only fueled my rage and frustration. How could this still be happening? How could a city like Chicago, with all its progress, still allow such reckless and discriminatory policing? How could I, a woman who had worked hard, followed the rules, and built a life for myself, be treated as though I didn't matter?

This wasn't just my story. It was the story of so many others who had suffered at the hands of a system that saw neighborhoods like mine as less deserving of dignity, respect, and basic human rights. And that realization pushed me even harder to demand justice.

As I paint the picture of how the police treated me in my neighborhood, I have to pause and reflect on those who cannot demand justice. Yes, I am a fighter; it's in my DNA, as we'll see in the next chapter. I am a professional social worker with a great network. Not everyone has the wherewithal to fight the Chicago Police Department or the City of Chicago. You need determination, you need strength, and you need to know that people actually believe you and support you. In order to do the type of fighting I did or even to find mere answers, you need resources. You need time. You need a sound mind. Many people I've spoken out for just don't have those things. It's not any fault of their own; it's the way it is. A system treats them like they don't matter or they are invisible? This is not right. This just doesn't sit well with me. This is not how things should be.

How was this raid fair? How was any botched raid on innocent people justice? Trauma never is fair, whether it is intentional or a mistake. But I've learned that somehow, someway, healing can happen whether or not you receive the answers you desire. To really heal—to try to influence what I could control—I dug deep into my DNA to find the resilience I needed to push past this pain. A little bit of coincidence and a lot of God's timing set me up in a place where I was thinking more and more about my grandmother. Little did I know I was really being set up to lean on my strong heritage to move past this pain.

What questions do you still have about the trauma you've endured? Do you think finding the answers will assist in your healing? Why or why not?

Advice from a Therapist

Alicia Troff-Meade, LCSW, discusses ways to move past cultural hindrances around therapy tools like taking medication.

When it comes to participating in therapy, clients from "minority backgrounds" have concerns about being judged or negatively perceived due to past discrimination. Therefore, they may have been influenced by their community to believe that therapy is unhelpful, while clients with a history of trauma may see therapy as just another avenue to experience re-traumatization. However, some of these beliefs are predicated on old history. Just as it's important for traumatized clients to remember "now" is not "then," minority clients need to remember that history and mass beliefs are always changing. And while their concerns are based on past experiences, it's a good idea to practice being flexible to new experiences and possibilities.

Many therapists have professional websites that give people an idea of their specialties, background, and training. The potential client should look at these websites as a first step. Clients should then give themselves permission to interview the therapist before committing to the process. Many therapists allow for one consultation in person or over the phone.

Being honest about your fears around cultural misunderstandings is an acceptable place to start. It is important for you to discuss your initial distrust of the therapeutic process. A good therapist who is well versed in working with multicultural clients will understand and empathize with these concerns. As a potential client, remember that you are the one seeking services; therefore, you are ultimately in control over which therapist you choose or whether or not you take medication.

All of your choices should feel empowering rather than intimidating or injuring. If that initial phone call or consultation creates increased feelings of intimidation or distrust, move on to another consultation with a second therapist, and so on until you feel you have a good fit and cultural competency is shown.

5

LUCENDIA'S GRANDBABY: THE FIGHT WAS IN MY DNA

I WAS BAPTIZED BY fire on that cold Chicago night of February 21, 2019. I didn't ask for it and I didn't deserve it, yet it happened, and it changed the course of my life. Something died inside of me. Yet, looking back now, I realize I was awakened to a new path and a new awareness of what was in me from my very conception. I found out that resilience was in my DNA. I'm not saying trauma always has a purpose, but what I've learned is that purpose certainly can emerge from dealing with your trauma—even if it's a new purpose that has been informed by your trauma. Dealing with the issues that are thrown upon you—and even those that you've participated in—can produce something you never knew you had; it can uncover different passions and different purposes.

I once heard a preacher share that purpose is what we are. I agree with what Sarah Jakes Roberts writes in her book *Power Moves*. She talks about purpose emerging from the stuff we've been through, and the way purpose shifts and evolves over time. Purpose is not something that we strive to reach. Rather, purpose is formed from who we are and what we've been through.

I understand it can be complicated and, quite frankly, disrespectful to see our purpose in the midst of our pain. I don't believe I should call out another person's purpose based on their pain. This can lead to further abuse of victims. But when the person who has been harmed finds their own purpose, I believe this can be a major part of their healing and set them on a path to victory over the pain. Purpose can emerge from all of the pain and tragedy. Purpose can surface from our trauma. And that can set us on an entirely different trajectory. There's great healing power in knowing that you're doing something purposeful, even with the mess that was handed to you in the form of trauma.

The end goal of dealing with trauma is healing, and that looks different for everyone. I hope and pray that you can find your path toward healing and see a new purpose unfold as I did—or, I should say, I am currently doing—along this journey. Remember that healing is a journey with many ebbs and flows and definitely not an exact destination.

Recalling the resilience and example of the woman who raised me—my grandmother, Lucendia—unknowingly helped me uncover my purpose after suffering the trauma that was thrust upon me. The night of the raid, after the associate pastor from my church left my apartment, I lay across my bed with tears flooding my pillowcase, replaying the unbelievable scene I had witnessed hours earlier. *What in the world just happened?* I thought over and over, alternating with only one other thought:

They are not going to get away with this. I'm Lucendia's grandbaby. I have to fight. Unbeknownst to me, I was articulating what would become my mantra. I just didn't know how true that statement was nor how my grandmother would help me fight.

I also didn't know how the work I was doing prior to the raid would assist in my discovery. More and more, I understand the meaning of Isaiah 55:8–9: "'For my thoughts are not your thoughts, neither are your ways my ways,' declares the Lord. 'As the heavens are higher than the earth, so are my ways higher than your ways and my thoughts than your thoughts.'"

Lucendia Young.

Turns out, the God I know and believe in was capable of stopping such a nightmare. The God I had questioned because the raid happened works at a different level than I do. Somehow, I believe God had orchestrated a project for me to work on just prior to this awful nightmare. And this project was aligned with what would emerge as my purpose and what would help me get through the devastating impact of the trauma.

I've dedicated my life to social work and helping others—that was a clear purpose for me once I began my career. And eventually as I approached my fifties, I realized I needed a retirement plan. I began to think through what I'd do when I stopped working regular hours. How would I retire? How would I support myself and continue to work within my passion? I believe this is important for women; we need to think ahead and plan ahead.

As I completed my master's degree, I had been thinking of creating a consulting business to pass along the experience and information I had garnered in the social work field throughout my years of working. I know many women in the field, and I believe I was called to encourage even more women of color to realize the possibilities available in the field. I think when people who look like us work to help others who happen to look like us, there's a better chance of success. We can relate and understand experiences that other people are just not familiar with. I wanted to extend some of the work I had already been doing in mentoring younger and newer social workers by serving as a resource and support to those new to the field.

Once I put plans into action to begin this business—an idea that came to me after finishing my second master's degree and getting my licensure—I moved full speed ahead to create Café Social Work. I wanted to get the consulting business up and running a few years before I retired from my full-time job.

This way, I could shift into the consulting business after I left the hospital, allowing myself more flexibility but also having an established business available to help others. I had set March 16, 2019, as my official launch date for the consulting business.

I had intentionally chosen this date because it was the birth date of the woman who shaped so much of who I am—my grandmother. I wanted to honor her in some way and thought launching my business on her birthday would be a great way to celebrate her memory. Prior to this, each February during Black History Month, I posted on social media history-making facts about my grandmother. I had plenty of information on her, some even published in books. But because I planned to do a slideshow at the business launch, I had been poring over even more information on her to share. I wanted everyone to know why she is my Black history hero.

My Own Black History Hero

When I was only three years old, I moved to Shelby, Mississippi, to live with my grandmother, whom I called Ma. Before then, my mom had tried her best to care for me in Chicago, but she was young herself. She had a hard time, and the big city wasn't always friendly to her. Caring for others was so natural to Ma that taking in another child was no big deal. And to me, it was an upgrade in living. I loved being with Ma and quickly called the wooden shotgun house on the dusty road my home. I happily lived there with Ma and my grandfather, Ira, whom I called Granddaddy. Ma took in my brother too, and a few other cousins lived in our house off and on.

Shelby sat in the heart of the Delta, a land of rich soil and resilient people. It was a place where the land gave freely, even when the world did not. The Delta's connection to water, particularly the Mississippi River, created fertile grounds, which helped with agricultural production. So the land has always been considered rich even if the people living on it were not. Some might have looked at our small town and called us poor, but I never saw it that way. We had everything we needed—right there in our house, in our yard, and in the love that surrounded us. Ma's yard was always full of life. Chickens clucked and scattered as we ran after them, laughing as they flapped just out of reach. The vegetable garden behind the house was a masterpiece of neat, thriving rows—crowder peas, butter beans, okra, cucumbers, and tomatoes—each plant tended with care, each harvest bringing more than enough to feed our family and others.

But what made Ma's garden special wasn't just what grew there—it was how she shared it. People from all over town would show up with empty buckets, and Ma would send them away with their buckets overflowing with fresh produce. She didn't ask for anything in return. She didn't turn anyone away. "Take whatever you need," she'd call out, waving them off before they could protest. She believed no one in or around Shelby would go hungry if she had anything to do with it.

Looking back, I realize we were rich in ways that truly mattered. The generosity Ma showed, the way she cared for our community, and the deep-rooted connection we had to the land—it was all a lesson. A lesson in abundance, in sharing, and in the power of looking out for one another. In a world that often measured wealth in dollars, Ma measured it in how many people she could help, and by that standard, we were never poor.

Ma and Granddaddy had already lived a lifetime together by the time I showed up down South: more than twenty-five years of marriage, nine children raised—four sons and five daughters, including my mother—and a home that had become the heart of our family. Ma's roots stretched back to Louisiana, but as the story goes, she moved to Mississippi with her sister when she was around eighteen. Not long after, sometime in the late 1930s, she met Granddaddy. His family owned land in Mississippi, and with that foundation, he built their home—a modest two-bedroom house that became a refuge for generations. It was the house where they raised their children and, eventually, where some of us grandkids found shelter, love, and discipline under Ma's watchful eye.

Today, that house still stands on our family land. Over time, my family built a more modern brick three-bedroom home on the same property, but the old house remains, a symbol of our history, our struggles, and our deep roots in that Mississippi soil. It's more than just a building; it's a testament to the lives lived within its walls, the laughter and lessons passed down, and the faith that carried us all through.

Back in the early 1970s, when I lived with Ma, our house sat just two doors down from our church, St. Peter's Rock Missionary Baptist Church. The proximity to the church wasn't just geographical—it was spiritual, emotional, and deeply embedded in our way of life. Church wasn't optional; it was the center of everything. Rain or shine, we showed up every Sunday morning, dressed in our best, ready to praise God. The service felt like it stretched on for hours, with fiery sermons, heartfelt prayers, and the kind of gospel singing that could shake your soul.

But the real blessing came after the service. As soon as the final "Amen" was spoken, the congregation didn't just go home—they came to Ma's house. It was an unspoken tradition, a gathering that felt as natural as breathing. Ma's house became an extension of the church itself, a place where the spirit of fellowship continued around a hot meal.

And oh, what a meal it was. Ma never turned anyone away from her dinner table either; she never worried about whether there was enough to go around. Somehow, there was always enough. She would lay out a feast of fried chicken, golden corn bread, slow-cooked greens, black-eyed peas, and whatever else she had prepared that day. The smell alone could make your stomach growl.

There was a system to it, though. The adults ate first—church elders, deacons, visitors from out of town—anyone who had come through the church doors that morning. The children, including me, had to wait. We stood in the doorway or hovered in the yard, impatiently watching the grown folks pile their plates with Ma's home-cooked food. But we knew better than to complain. This was Ma's rule, and you didn't argue with Ma. We knew there was always enough—somehow. So we waited with much anticipation.

By the time it was finally our turn, the food still seemed endless. No matter how many people had come through, Ma always made sure everyone was fed. No one left her home hungry. Looking back, I marvel at how she did it—how she managed to cook for an entire congregation, serve with grace, and never seem exhausted by the effort. She didn't just feed people; she nourished them, body and soul.

That kind of generosity, that unwavering commitment to community, was at the core of who Ma was. She was providing comfort, extending hospitality, and ensuring that no one in our small Mississippi town ever felt alone. She knew, as so many Black women of her generation did, that survival wasn't just about making it through hard times—it was about lifting each other up in the process.

Ma's giving spirit didn't end with food. She was a caretaker, a listener, a problem solver. People came to her for advice, for encouragement, for the kind of wisdom that only someone who had lived through the struggles of the South could offer. She had seen it all—segregation, poverty, hard labor in the cotton fields—and yet she carried herself with a quiet dignity that made people trust her. She didn't have much in terms of money or material wealth, but what she had, she gave freely.

And it wasn't just people from the church who came to Ma's house. Strangers would stop by—travelers passing through, neighbors who had fallen on hard times. She welcomed them all. She believed in the simple but profound idea that everyone deserved kindness.

I didn't always appreciate it back then. As a child, I sometimes resented the long hours at church, the endless Sundays spent serving instead of playing. I wanted to be outside, running with my friends, not washing dishes after the congregation had eaten. But as I grew older, I began to understand. What Ma was teaching me wasn't just about tradition; it was about purpose.

She showed me what it meant to serve others, to lead not with words but with actions. She demonstrated that faith wasn't just something you practiced in church—it was something you lived every single day. Watching her, I learned that true strength isn't loud or boastful; it's steady, it's persistent, and it's rooted in love.

Those lessons never left me. They shaped the way I see the world, the way I fight for justice, the way I advocate for those who have been silenced. When I think about the work I do now as a result of a wrongful raid on my home—standing up for victims of police violence, pushing for reforms, demanding accountability—I see Ma's influence in all of it. She didn't just teach me to stand up for what's right; she showed me how to do it with grace, resilience, and an unwavering commitment to community. When people ask me how I had it in me to fight the big-city system of Chicago and its police force, I reflect on Ma. She wouldn't have stood for anything less. She was a fighter. I had to fight. I was Lucendia's baby, so there was nothing else I could do. In my tears, with my fear and anger, I just had to fight.

Even now, all these years later, I can still hear her voice on her land in Mississippi. "Take what you need," she'd say, waving someone off as they tried to refuse her generosity. It was never about having plenty—it was about making sure everyone had enough.

And maybe that's the greatest lesson she taught me: That we are all responsible for one another. That true abundance comes not from what we keep, but from what we give.

Sunday wasn't the only time our home served as a central gathering place. I still remember our phone ringing and Ma telling me to go down the street and get a neighbor. The phone call could be for Miss Betty or for someone at the Palmers' home a few doors down. We were the only family with a phone for several miles, and Ma welcomed others to share ours.

Ma didn't just serve the community through her meals, homegrown produce, or even phone service; she also stepped up and helped organize community-wide giveaways. She was a founding member of a co-op in the Delta. This group organized food distribution from the fields of Mississippi to the homes of its poorest residents. The group eventually began giving away clothes too.

While I never heard Ma even talk about finishing high school, she was on our town's school board and led voter registration drives in the 1960s. She stood up and spoke for what she believed in even among people with much more education than she had. Her hospitality shone through again when she and a group of other advocates, including well-known activist Fannie Lou Hamer, met in Ma's home to discuss ways to help Black people register to vote, even though it was dangerous. She went from house to house, encouraging people to register to vote. To me as a kid, these stories seemed normal; it was what Ma did. I didn't realize just how much courage and care it took for her to sacrifice her time and even risk her life for what she believed was right and just.

My Uncle Joseph once told her, "Ma, you going to get us killed," because she wouldn't stand down. She simply replied, "Son, if you don't stand for something, you going to die for anything."

Ma, who was called Big Lou by her friends in the community, encouraged others to push through obstacles for their rights and others' rights, even though the law said they weren't even supposed to be meeting. She boldly and faithfully worked for any cause she believed in, and she marched with Dr. King and others for those rights. She couldn't stand injustice, according to Joseph, her youngest son. She told the White people in power in the Delta, "If you all can have it, we can have it too . . . we ought to have access to it." To her, "it" was everything—from paved roads to streetlights—and she was willing to fight for it.

In the mid-1960s, a group of people who were already a part of the co-op that gave away food and clothing collaborated on a project spearheaded by social scientists and medical professionals from Tufts University to obtain a grant from President Lyndon Johnson's Office of Economic Opportunity. They established the Tufts-Delta Health Center in Mound Bayou, Mississippi, which was about eight miles down the road from Ma's house. They wanted to start a health center, but they did not want to just drop in and put a Band-Aid on some wounds and move on. They wanted to train the community to work at the center and care for each other. My grandmother was one of the first to sign up for training; she believed in the work as well as the philosophy of "teaching a man to fish" as a means to showing people how to care for themselves and others.

My grandmother trained with Tufts and fittingly became a nursing assistant. At dawn each morning, she would leave our home in her blue nurse's dress, pristinely ironed, with her gleaming white shoes that I was responsible for cleaning. She was proud and pleased to continue to serve her community through her medical training, but she still took care of her family. When we woke up, we'd find our breakfast waiting on us. The eggs and homemade biscuits were still warm. And when we got back home after school, Ma had trained us to do our homework and then we could eat the supper she had left on the stove. Ma was a superb cook, and I loved her pinto beans, white northern beans, black-eyed peas, butter beans, and crowder peas. (To this day, I won't eat beans; I had my share of them growing up.) Her garden's yield never went to waste as she'd wash them, precook them, and then place those vegetables in bags to be frozen and pulled out during winter or when the harvest was done. She canned her own fruit and preserves.

It's in My DNA

Ma wasn't the kind of grandmother who showed affection through hugs and kisses. She wasn't one to fuss over us with soft words or coddling. Instead, she loved through service. Her long arms were not used to pull me into tight embraces; rather, they were used to cook meals for those in need, to clean the church, to work in the garden, and to care for anyone who crossed her path. Love, for her, was an action. And because of that, we—her grandchildren—were taught to serve as well.

She made sure we understood that helping others wasn't just a good thing to do, it was a way of life. I remember so many evenings when Ma would cook extra food, pack it up, and send us kids to deliver it to someone in the community. It didn't matter if they were sick, struggling, or simply alone—if Ma knew they needed a hot meal, they got one. And we were the ones carrying her love, plate by plate, from our house to theirs. We were her own little personal delivery service—well before Grubhub or Uber Eats were ever thought of.

But it wasn't just her actions that introduced me to the true love of God—it was the way she spoke to Jesus as if He were sitting right beside her that caught my attention. I knew something was different about her and that she had a genuine relationship with God through Christ.

Ma didn't just pray on Sunday at church. She prayed all the time. She prayed while cooking, while sweeping the porch, while picking vegetables from the garden. Sometimes, she prayed so casually that it felt like she was just having a conversation with an old friend. "Sweet Jesus, you see me trying to get this bread to rise, help me out now," she'd say as she kneaded dough. Or, "Lord, keep these babies safe today," as we ran out the door to play. She embodied Paul's words in 1 Thessalonians 5:17: "Pray without ceasing." Prayer was a part of her life. She had a constant conversation going with her Lord, and she meant every word she shared.

If she wasn't talking to Jesus, she was humming about Him. Music filled our house, and with it, His name consistently floated through the airwaves. The record player was always spinning, playing the rich, soulful voices of her favorite gospel artists—Mahalia Jackson, James Cleveland, the Five Blind Boys of Alabama. Their voices wrapped around our home like a warm blanket, reminding us of a "Precious Lord" who could take us by the hand; telling us that "God Is" as we heard that God truly is the one who "moves all pain, misery, and doubt"; and proclaiming that Ma was "Living for My Jesus," right along with the harmonizing group. Even when the record player wasn't on, Ma was humming, always humming. Sometimes it was an old spiritual, sometimes it was a hymn, but always, always, Jesus's name was in her moan or her song.

At the time, I didn't fully understand the depth of her faith. I just knew that Jesus was everywhere in our home—on her lips, in her songs, in her actions. And though I may not have recognized it then, those moments—watching her pray, listening to her hum, delivering food to strangers—were shaping me. She didn't just tell me about Jesus; she showed me Jesus through her love, her service, and her unwavering faith. And for that, I am forever grateful.

I've always been very proud of my heritage. Anyone who knows me knows I will gladly share a story about my grandmother and Mississippi. I was and still am very proud of my grandmother's work in our community and how she shaped me. But I had never really put together how what I witnessed as a child in Shelby had shaped my desire to help others. Now, as I processed my next move while trying to heal from the trauma inflicted on me, it became clear that my grandma's influence was not in vain. In watching her compassionate activism as I grew up, I didn't realize I was being trained to become an advocate and community organizer myself.

Me in a Mississippi cotton field.

I got my fight from my grandmother. It was a part of my history and my destiny. And now, in the aftermath of the trauma I endured on February 21, 2019, that spark was being ignited. Yes, I had been a social worker caring for the needs of the people in the city of my birth, but now I felt pushed into a deeper place. As I grappled with what happened to me, I had to dig into the lessons I learned from the small community Ma raised me in and served faithfully. This was part of my 360 moment. I had returned to Chicago as an adult, but the lessons I picked up in Mississippi would prepare me to fight the biggest battle of my life. They would prepare me to stand up to mayors, stand with mayors, speak to the press, tell the public, keep fighting a big-city system, and demand change. My fight has now extended to Springfield, Illinois, where the state legislature meets. I've proposed an ordinance and met with representatives and senators there. The fight has taken me to Washington, DC, too. This fight may have started in my apartment in the West Loop of Chicago, but it will not end there. It is bigger than me, and I feel empowered to seek the change I desire.

Slowly, as I dug into my grandmother's story while preparing to honor her through my work as a consultant with Café Social Work, I began to see my purpose in a much broader context. I thought of others whose voices have been stripped from them and who cannot fight back against a system that recklessly destroys their lives and leaves without fixing what lies broken in its wake. I read about their stories. As I became more involved in advocating for change in Chicago, I had the opportunity to work with Service Employees International Union Healthcare Illinois and Indiana (SEIU HCII), a union committed to social justice and community empowerment. Through our collaboration, we conducted research on the frequency and impact of wrongful police raids across the city. What we uncovered was both alarming and deeply unjust.

The data revealed that multiple dangerous and dehumanizing raids occur in Chicago every single day. In 2019 alone, there were at least 1,334 police raids—an astonishing number that highlights the aggressive and often reckless approach law enforcement took in executing search warrants. More disturbingly, these raids were not distributed evenly across the city. Black and Brown neighborhoods were disproportionately targeted, with far more frequent and invasive police actions compared to predominantly White areas.

These wrongful raids aren't just statistics—they represent real families and individuals who had their homes violently invaded, their dignity stripped away, and their sense of safety shattered. Many innocent residents, including children, were subjected to terrifying encounters with heavily armed officers, often based on faulty information or mistaken identities. The trauma inflicted by these raids extends beyond the immediate moment, leaving lasting emotional and psychological scars on those affected.

This research reinforced what many in our communities already knew firsthand—that systemic racism and discriminatory policing were deeply embedded in Chicago's law enforcement practices. It further fueled my commitment to pushing for meaningful reform, ensuring that no one else would have to endure the same violations of trust and human rights that so many had suffered. The fight for justice wasn't just necessary, it was urgent.

Like me, these people figuratively have their door propped shut with an ironing board because the system barged in and left that door broken. Who stands up for them? Because of February 21, 2019, I had been summoned to be a voice for people. I was being called to channel the strength and heart of my grandmother to serve people in a different way.

I just so happened to be ready to launch Café Social Work into the world with a presentation about the woman who inspired me the most. Because I was determined not to let the 2019 raid take away this dream, I pressed on to launch the business just a few weeks after my life had been ransacked. Little did I know that the preparation for this launch—continuing to pore over documents about Ma's work and her own social work café (even if not incorporated as a business) and think about all she gave and did—was readying me for a much bigger assignment. I was recalling what I was made of in preparation for my next phase of life. I thought it would be one thing, but God made it even bigger.

I believe the seeds for our paths and purpose are often planted in early childhood experiences. We do not realize it, because naturally we're too young to understand how the puzzle pieces of our lives fit together. We are merely observing, not realizing we are being crafted for our life work.

I think about Moses. He was born an Israelite during a tumultuous time for his people (Exodus 1:22–2:3). There was a hit on his life when he was born. He was not supposed to grow up; he was not supposed to see age two. Yet in God's providence, his life was spared. He was sheltered in Pharaoh's home yet raised by his biological mother under the disguise of a slave girl servant to Pharaoh's daughter. Surely Moses's mother's prayers, songs, and actions shaped the man who would become a liberator for his people. Even as he partook in Pharaoh's food and culture, a seed was planted inside him that gave him a special heart and passion for Israel. He used this passion, though reluctantly, to stand up and find a voice to free God's people, to free his people.

I also think about Joseph's story in Genesis when I think about purpose. Although Joseph's story has long resonated with me, I see more and more correlations between his story and my own. Early in Joseph's story, he has had a dream that one day his brothers will bow down to him (Genesis 37:5–11). Bible students know how Joseph's story ends—it's definitely not one straight line toward the realization of his dream. No, Joseph goes through the traumatic experiences of being thrown in a pit by his very own brothers, sold into Egyptian slavery, falsely accused of sexual harassment, and thrown into jail with forgotten promises. Yet Joseph's purpose emerged even in the midst of all he had been through. His dream became a reality. And the beautiful part about it is that he didn't allow the experiences he had been through to make him bitter. (See his proclamation in Genesis 50:20: "You intended to harm me, but God intended it for good to accomplish what is now being done, the saving of many lives.")

And that's what I take away from February 21, 2019. It was my worst nightmare lived out in real time. Yet, because I worked to honor my grandmother despite that night, I discovered her resilience and all the lessons she had poured into me about working tirelessly to help others and bring about justice. I picked up her mantle and ran with it. I became like Joseph, determined to stay focused on what was right even when wrong was all around me. I have to admit, I didn't always realize that healing was occurring; that's how it is. Focus on something else, something good and noble (for some help, see Philippians 4:8), and the healing will emerge, along with a purpose that goes beyond yourself, one that helps others.

Trust me, I know it is hard to see past the circumstances and trauma that may have broken you and soaked your pillow in tears, but dare I say that looking deeper can show you signs that may point to your destiny too. Who have you been called to liberate? Who have you been called to give voice to? Whose story may be released through your story? If you're uncertain of the answer, I encourage you to reflect on the home or circumstances you grew up in. Whether your early life was traumatic, or loving like mine, the seeds may have been planted to produce the person and passion that exist today. February 21, 2019, was the baptism that uncovered my desire to fight for justice and equality for others—just like Lucendia had done before my very eyes at her home on the dirt road in Shelby, Mississippi. Remembering her gave me the needed push to keep moving forward when everything inside of me really wanted to stop and crumble. Have you been baptized by fire into a new path and purpose?

After much thought, prayer, and even therapy, I've decided not to make what was done to me the end of my story. I didn't want it, but since it has happened, I will redeem this story to grow into my purpose. As the reporter Dave Savini puts it, "Anjanette is not giving up, and I applaud her. It is fulfilling for me to watch her evolution. She has become a mother to all those kids who had guns pointed at them or saw their parents held at gunpoint in raids."

I appreciate Dave's word: *evolution*. I have become a different person because of the raid. And I have become much more empathetic toward anyone, especially a child, who has to go through a similar situation because of the police culture and mindset toward people of color in this city and nation. As I think about this journey, however, I've decided to remind myself that trauma is what happened to me, but I am not my trauma. I'm so much more than a botched raid. But I'm using that raid to step more and more into my purpose. I'm emerging. Like Moses, I have taken on the voice for those who cannot speak. I am Lucendia's grandbaby.

Are you at the point where you can see new purpose emerging after your trauma? If so, begin to journal about it and the ways that you have evolved. If not, it is OK. Living out your journey has a way of revealing what is needed when it is needed most.

Advice from a Therapist

Alicia Troff-Meade, LCSW, answers the question: How can reflecting on your childhood help you heal?

All of us are born with a purpose. We don't understand this as children, but our path is one of growth, and the experiences that we create expand consciousness. Our individual purpose exists outside of comfortable or uncomfortable, good or bad. Therefore, at a certain point during adulthood, we instinctively begin to ask ourselves, *Why am I here? What am I meant to learn in this lifetime?* Until we answer this, our lives may feel pointless or meaningless.

One way we can begin to understand our purpose is to reflect on all the experiences we've had up to this point, looking for patterns, themes, repetitions. This is why it's valuable to explore the events of one's childhood. In doing so, we will find the patterns, themes, and repetitions that point to our purpose. Some of us are busy exploring the idea of extremes to learn about balance. As we reflect on our experiences, we may notice patterns that point to many ups and downs in our life. Some of us are exploring conflict to understand the nature of cooperation, so we'll notice many experiences of friction in our relationships. Others are exploring the concept of beauty, physical strength, or illness to understand the mechanism of physicality, so the car accident that created their disfigurement and the sick child they took care of as a mother or father will be the tools of understanding.

The themes you uncover throughout your life will point to your purpose. There are countless possible themes, but you will begin to see one main theme that feels like your purpose.

When you find it, your perceptions will change as you relax in that knowledge. The entirety of your life will make sense. You will no longer see yourself as a victim of misfortune but as an excellent creator. You won't judge your experiences or put blame on yourself or others. You'll embrace your experiences with the understanding that your life was not about failing to be good enough or smart enough or worthy. You've simply been exploring your purpose, and these experiences were your lessons.

6

JUSTICE, SUPPORT, AND THE CHURCH

I'VE HEARD PEOPLE—BOTH Christians and those who are not—criticize the church for various reasons. Some do it because they have endured real hurt and even trauma from people in the church. That, however, is not my experience, thank God. I can say without a doubt that my church, Progressive Baptist Church on the South Side of Chicago, was—and continues to be—one of the greatest resources I could possibly have during such a traumatic time in my life. Everything I needed, God provided through my church.

Progressive Baptist Church, which has decades of history being a beacon of hope to the community, sits prominently on the side of the Dan Ryan Expressway that runs south from the city's Loop. Large pictures of past pastors are etched on a sign in front of its building, providing just a glimpse of its remarkable history. Its towering presence over the city is more than just a structure—it is a symbol of resilience, refuge, and righteous defiance. When I think of Progressive Baptist Church, I think of a place that held me, strengthened me, and reminded me that standing up for what is right is woven into its very foundation.

Progressive Baptist Church was founded in 1918 at 3652 S. Dearborn Street and is fondly known as "the church that moved across the expressway." But it is much more than that. It is a church that stood its ground—literally and figuratively—against the City of Chicago.

In May 1958, the city announced plans to develop an expressway project that would require demolishing the church. Reverend T. E. Brown refused to allow it. He and the congregation did not bow to the city's demands. Instead, they fought back. They negotiated, they resisted, and ultimately, they won. The city agreed to move the entire church—lifting it off its foundation and transporting it, block by block, to its current location at 3658 S. Wentworth Avenue. This relocation became the largest structural move in Chicago's history, and more important, it became a testament to the power of a community unwilling to be erased. Yes, Progressive is truly the church that moved across the expressway, and ever since hearing its history, I can't help but smile a bit more seeing the huge building looming over the Dan Ryan. Its very building is a testament to resilience, advocacy, and uniting with one voice.

When I reflect on my own battle with the City of Chicago after the wrongful raid on my home, I realize that the spirit of resistance was always in the walls of that church. The same unwavering faith that saved Progressive Baptist Church in 1958 was the faith that carried me through my fight for justice. It is no coincidence that this church became my place of refuge, my source of strength. When I stood against the city, demanding accountability for the trauma inflicted upon me, I was walking in the footsteps of those who had stood before me. Just as Rev. Brown refused to let the city destroy his church, I refused to let my story be buried, my pain ignored, or my humanity disregarded.

Progressive Baptist Church taught me that resistance is not just about defying oppression—it is also about knowing your worth, your power, and your right to exist in spaces where others may try to push you out. The people of this church wrapped their arms around me, supported me, and reinforced what I already knew in my heart: fighting back is in our history, and it is in our future. The fight for justice is never easy. It requires boldness, resilience, and a belief that change is possible—even when the odds are against you. But I stand today, just as Progressive Baptist Church stood over six decades ago, knowing that when we refuse to be moved by injustice, we become the force that moves the world forward.

Looking back, I realize God was in this place of refuge and had sent me to this place before my traumatic night. I had been a faithful member at another church in the south suburbs of Chicago for many years; it was near where I once lived and raised my son. It was my family church. But when I moved into the city, I eventually thought I needed a church near my home in the city for several reasons. I began to pray.

I had only been a member of Progressive for three years before my nightmare. I "courted" this church for a few months back in 2015, visiting its early morning service before attending my other church's services. I found it by simply doing a Google search for Baptist churches in Chicago. I like to jokingly (but also seriously) say that I was born a Baptist, raised a Baptist, and desired to stay in the Baptist denomination. The first church that popped up in my random search was Progressive, so I clicked on its site. I listened to several sermons from the pastor, Charlie Dates, and I was inspired. The messages were Bible based and made me think more about God and Scripture. I was intrigued and before I knew it, several hours had passed and I was still listening to his sermons streaming on my computer. Coincidentally, I found out that Progressive was located near the highway and I passed it every Sunday as I drove to my previous church in the suburbs before I became a member there. It had a rich history steeped in the history of African Americans who migrated from the South and settled in this big city in the Midwest.

It's probably not a coincidence that Progressive felt like my family. When I visited the church, I sat next to a few legacy members (older women) who embraced me and loved on me and treated me like family. This was attractive to me and made me feel at home even as a visitor. I later developed a loving and enduring relationship with one of the women, "Sis. Taylor," who embraced me as her daughter in Christ until the day she died.

By the beginning of 2016, I decided my dating days were over and I would commit to this church. One of my New Year's resolutions was to join Progressive. I talked with the officers at my former church and let them know why I would be leaving. I had been in leadership at that church and wanted to leave on a good note, in what my Baptist roots would call "good standing." I thought it was only right to share with my pastor and team that I was leaving this church because I was being drawn to Progressive and not because of anything against this church.

One of the first things I recall when I joined Progressive was the new member classes. These weekly classes, which I took for two months, really made me feel connected to the church and its members. I was ready to serve at my new church because that's how I was raised: you don't just go to church, you serve;

you don't just take from the church's worship experience, you give back to God's people in whatever way you are gifted to. This is what my grandmother had taught me through her words and her example. I remember Rev. Ray (the angel who showed up to console me at my apartment on the night of the raid) teaching us about Progressive as the leader of the new member classes. I remember telling him that it was important to me that I not get lost in this church, which had several hundred more people than my other church. I didn't want to just be another number or another person in the pew. I stayed close to the other people in my cohort, those who joined the church when I did and went through the new member classes with me.

Interestingly enough, as I was saying that I needed to serve in my new church, the pastor of the church, Pastor Charlie, singled me out and asked me to help restructure the usher board. How he chose me, I'm not sure. I hadn't served as an usher before, but he shared with me his vision of having the ministry become more of a greeters' ministry, one spreading hospitality to people as they entered the building. He thought this was a perfect fit for me based on his observations of me over the past few months. He said he thought I'd be able to connect and serve people well. Being new to Progressive, I may have been able to bring new insight into how to welcome people.

Pastor Charlie says he remembered seeing that I was eager to engage immediately with the church. He could tell I wanted to be involved in the life of the church. So you don't let an eager member sit idly; you help them find the best place for their gifts. He was happy to place me in what would become our hospitality ministry to improve the church's front-facing presentation. He wanted members and visitors to feel more warmth when they entered our sanctuary, and he thought I was the type of person to bring this out in others.

A bit surprised that I, a new member, would be helping in this area, I agreed to help in any way I could. I had been taught to serve. The Mississippi house I grew up in sat just two doors down from the church we attended, and my grandmother—always with me in tow—was the first to arrive and the last to leave. Whether it was cleaning on Saturdays, opening the doors for Sunday school, or making sure everything was locked up afterward, she was committed.

As a child, I didn't always appreciate it. I would have much rather been outside playing with my friends than spending countless hours at church. But looking back now, I'm deeply grateful that she made me go. Those moments instilled in me a profound sense of service—one that has shaped who I am today.

Through serving in this ministry group, I got to know people quickly. I was often one of the first faces they saw as they entered our sanctuary. I tried to make sure people felt welcomed. I developed many personal connections.

When I took a step back and reflected on my healing journey, I was amazed to realize that every resource I needed to begin making real progress had come from Progressive. What struck me most was how, years ago, I had been led to this very church without knowing just how profoundly it would shape my path. At the time, I had no idea that the relationships I built and the faith I nurtured within those walls would one day become my lifeline. Looking back, I can see the undeniable hand of God guiding me to exactly where I needed to be.

The night of the raid—the most traumatic night of my life—Progressive was there for me in ways I never could have imagined. Rev. Ray was one of the first people to comfort me, offering words of reassurance that reminded me I wasn't alone. In the early hours of Friday morning, as I struggled to process what had just happened, I spoke with Pastor Charlie. His presence, his prayers, and his unwavering support anchored me in the midst of my fear and confusion. At a time when everything felt chaotic and uncertain, the people God had placed in my life through this church became my steady foundation.

But it wasn't just the pastors who showed up. My attorney, my prayer partner, my sister in Christ—all of them rallied around me, offering guidance, encouragement, and the kind of love that only God can provide. In those moments, I experienced firsthand what it truly means for the church to be the church. It wasn't about a building, a sermon, or a Sunday service—it was about a community of believers who embodied the love and compassion of Christ in the most tangible way possible.

Through their presence, I saw the power of faith in action. They didn't just offer words of comfort; they stood by me, fought for me, and prayed over me. They became the hands and feet of Jesus in my time of greatest need. It was through them that I found not only healing but also strength to keep going, to seek justice, and to refuse to let this experience break me.

What amazes me most is how God had been orchestrating this support system long before I even knew I would need it. Years ago, when I first walked through the doors of Progressive, I simply thought I was finding a church home. I had no idea I was stepping into a divine safety net that would one day catch me when I felt like I was falling.

This experience reinforced what I have always believed: God's provision is always on time. Even in the darkest moments, He places the right people in our lives to remind us that we are not alone. The church showed up as the church, and because of that, I was able to walk through one of the hardest moments of my life with faith, hope, and the unwavering knowledge that I was deeply loved.

As I mentioned, in the aftermath of the raid, Keenan immediately began working on my case, determined to hold the city accountable for what had happened to me. One of the first major steps we took was meeting with the mayor, a conversation that came shortly after the video of the raid was made public and I held my first press conference. That press conference was a defining moment—I finally had the chance to share my story, not just with the media but with the entire city. The weight of what had happened to me was no longer only my burden to carry; it was now a matter of public concern.

During the press conference, I spoke directly to the mayor and reminded her of something significant—she had campaigned at my church, standing before my congregation, asking for our votes and promising to be a leader who would fight for justice. Now, I wanted her to return to my church, look me in the eye, and tell me exactly how she planned to make things right. I wanted her to address not just me but also my community, and take real responsibility for what had happened.

Unfortunately, that meeting was nothing short of disappointing. Just hours before we were scheduled to sit down with the mayor, her staff sent over a lengthy chain of e-mails that revealed something deeply troubling: She had been made aware of my wrongful raid when it first happened. Yet, despite knowing about the trauma I endured, she had chosen to do nothing. No outreach. No acknowledgment. No effort to correct the harm that had been done.

Sitting across from her, I saw firsthand what so many people had already suspected: her concern was not about justice or accountability, but about damage control. That meeting ended with empty words and a false promise from the mayor to "make things right." But as time went on, it became painfully clear that those words carried no real weight.

After several failed attempts to negotiate with the city and push for meaningful action, Keenan decided that a stronger approach was necessary. He sent a formal demand letter—not as a legal threat, but as a communication designed to force the city to finally pay attention and engage in real discussions with us. The goal wasn't just compensation; it was acknowledgment, accountability, and a commitment to preventing this from happening to anyone else.

At every turn, we were met with resistance. The city dragged its feet, offering half-hearted responses and bureaucratic obstacles instead of real solutions. But I refused to be silenced. This wasn't just about me—it was about every Black and Brown resident who had been subjected to wrongful raids, every family whose home had been violently invaded, and every person who had been treated as a criminal simply because of where they lived.

The fight for justice was only beginning, but one thing was clear—I was not backing down. I had a team behind me, a community that supported me, and a voice that was finally being heard.

Then in 2020 our world was shut down by COVID, bringing things to a halt as the courts closed. I'd already been fired from my job and was shifting into my new one. I was depressed and overwhelmed. I needed my church. I needed help. I needed something stable in my life, so I asked Pastor Charlie if I could attend services even though the church was shut down. Charlie agreed. The pastor and a small team helping to stream the service were still showing up at church each Sunday and I was allowed to attend too. I stood at the door, going through the motions of my hospitality duties even though we were not open. This routine became such a healing balm for me. I cherished the music, the messages, and the small encounters with those working for the service. Everything I needed was right there at Progressive, praise God. My life had been forever altered, and I was just trying to make it, somehow.

I often say, "I didn't lose my life that night the police raided my apartment, but I lost a lot of my life that night." I was walking through life numb, depressed, a shell of the woman I had been prior to February 2019. But I found a way to keep moving one step at a time. Going to the building at my church each Sunday was a big part of that process. I didn't realize it at the time, but getting up every Sunday morning really made a difference. I had a reason to take a shower, to put on clothes, to put on makeup, and to do something when I was at one of the lowest points after this ridiculous ordeal. By this time, I had been suffering silently for a year, and now I was in forced isolation with the rest of the world. My case was at a standstill because of the pandemic, and no one—not one of those twelve men who busted my door down and intruded on my home and life—had been brought to justice. I was suffering and at rock bottom. But each Sunday I stood at my post as a greeter to a virtual congregation, and that helped me make it through one more day and one more week. I had a purpose. I needed to do this to keep going and survive. Attending church with just eight other team members running the live stream was a lifeline. I needed the routine. I needed the spiritual renewal I felt walking through those doors. I needed my church, and once again, my church provided.

My therapist, Alicia Troff-Meade, says routine can help by giving those recovering from trauma a sense of control and predictability; this sense of predictability can help in reducing anxiety and fostering a sense of stability and safety. A person who lives with trauma does not feel safe, does not see the world as predictable, and doesn't feel in control. Thus, having moments of feeling safe, secure, and trusting can be very healing. Visiting a healing, comforting place often is a good way to push past the pain and find wholeness and help with continuing on the journey. It can take time to recognize your comfort place. One way to find a place is to pay attention to your body and your emotions. Make note of the places where you feel joy or where you don't feel anxious. What places do you desire to go to?

Early in that first year after the raid, many people in my church had no idea what I had been through. I had only told my close family and friends and my boss about what happened to me. Of course, my pastor and his staff knew, along with my attorney, but that was pretty much it. As recounted in the previous chapter, when the first story about this raid showed up on the news, we couldn't use any of the video footage—we hadn't been allowed to even see it yet. The city denied our FOIA requests. So that first story didn't get much attention. It probably wasn't until my first press conference after the second story aired with the body cam video that people recognized me and knew what I had been through.

I held many of my press conferences at Progressive, and attorneys serving in the social justice and counseling ministry at my church showed up for each of them. They came to city council meetings with me to stand by my side and be a support. It was a wonderful feeling to be surrounded by church members. I knew they had my back. I knew they loved me and supported me. Everything I needed was in Progressive.

The women from our women's ministry started checking in on me and praying with me. They gave me so much support when they realized what I was going through. I'm not sure how I would have made it through without their love and care and concern. They were exactly what I needed even though I had no clue what I needed.

My church has been and continues to be a big part of my healing journey. If it had not been for my church, I would not have gotten all the help I needed. I know that without a doubt.

And for me, I kept showing up. On those rough days, the lonely days, the days I fell deeper and deeper into depression, I showed up to my church. I think this ability to keep showing up came from my grandmother too. When we got older and were able to hang out on Saturday nights, I still remember her loud voice reminding us, "I don't care what time you come home on Saturday night, you getting up and going to church on Sunday morning." And that's exactly what we did. Forming that habit early in my life became a saving grace in the months after the raid.

One Sunday a while after the raid (because when you've been through trauma, your life is demarcated by before and after the incident), I heard my pastor at Progressive preach from Isaiah 9:1–5. He said, "In your darkest moments, the church should be there to reach out a hand to you." He was referring to the prophetic message of the Old Testament prophet Isaiah, who told the people who were in a very, very dark place at the time that they would see a great light. Some scholars call this light a foreshadowing of Christ. When Christ came on earth, the darkness was overtaken by light. His purpose and mission were to bring salvation to a lost people. His very nature and work brought light in dark places. He overshadowed the darkness with his light.

Isaiah 9:2 specifically says, "The people who walked in darkness have seen a great light; those who dwelt in the land of the shadow of death, upon them a light has shined." The church serves as the body of Christ, so they should be the very light for the dark world, a tangible representation of Christ on earth. The church should be what shines brightest in the darkest and gloomiest hour. The church shows the dark world Christ. The church is the hands and feet of Christ, doing the work of spreading and sharing the light in the midst of darkness.

When Pastor Charlie preached this passage, so eloquently breaking down Isaiah 9, I realized he wasn't just preaching from the Bible and about the Bible. He was actually describing my church and what Progressive Baptist Church was for me. My church was actually doing this in my life at that time. My church was living out what God said in the Bible. I experienced it fully. My church showed up for me as I lived through the darkest, worst nightmare; my church showed up as a lifeline and as pure light for me in the dark. I don't know where I'd be without their light shining in my life. Certainly, I'd still be bumbling around in the dark, trying to figure out why and how this happened. Who knows to what depths my depression would have continued to sink if my church hadn't been such a needed light to me.

Pastor Charlie humbly says that he isn't sure Progressive ministered to me perfectly, but he is certain that they did operate as a team, which I believe is just as important. My church was with me, from the lawyers down to the church members praying for me. Pastor Charlie calls it "wraparound care," where all parts of the church take care of those in need in a loving, holistic, and comprehensive way. I'm so very grateful I was able to experience this.

I even shared with the congregation after that message that our church is truly doing what it is called to do. We were soliciting donations for the justice center, and I was days away from making the announcement about my settlement with the city (more on that later). I proudly stood before the congregation and shared that Progressive had showed up for me. I told them that when they saw me on the news this very week, they should know that their church was responsible for what occurred. I said when you hear what has happened this week, you should know that your church was the one that got me here. I was not just speaking of the financial outcome from the settlement, I was also speaking about that wraparound care that was by my side the night of the raid through this very day, attending press conferences, praying over me, allowing me to attend service during the pandemic, and so much more I can't even describe.

I know everyone's experiences have not been so positive with churches even—or perhaps especially—when healing from trauma. I think this is unfortunate; after all, a church is called to be a healing place. I've heard ministers claim the church is a hospital for the sick, both physically and spiritually. If this is the case, shouldn't there be opportunities and places to truly heal? I sincerely wish everyone healing from trauma could have the experience I had at Progressive. Perhaps you can find that comfort and light in a church or maybe another group that can be a comforting place where you can process and mend and feel loved and supported—all settings ripe to help mend your heart, body, and soul.

Healing is very much done in community, Camille Quinn tells me. "You can't heal in a vacuum." People need space to process what they have endured and are enduring. When we heal, she says, "we regain a sense of urgency. . . . You can say,

'I have some control over my life and what it is and what is not happening to me.'" While the past harms do not go away, you can develop a level of capacity to self-soothe. And then you can say, "I'm not going to let this wreck my spirit." Healing is a gift to yourself.

In the foreword to Natasha Smith's book *Black Woman Grief: A Guide to Hope and Wholeness*, Quantrilla Ard writes, "Community is one of the greatest helps in grief. The desire to hide our grief in a world that makes us feel 'othered' is normal—however, we are not meant to go on this journey alone. We need each other."

I had no clue what I was getting from Progressive when I joined my church, nor did I realize I was actually following a much-needed routine and embracing my small community during the pandemic when I made my way to the church. I didn't realize that my community was indeed helping me to heal. This makes sense, as research tells us that community is essential in effectively and sustainably "reducing the impact of trauma on families and societies."

To this day, Progressive is a balm for me. During a recent Black History Month celebration, the media ministry compiled a touching video showcasing the likes of Thurgood Marshall, Jesse Jackson Jr., and Rosa Parks to the melody of the Negro National Anthem, "Lift Every Voice and Sing." The video also included several shots of me, highlighting my fight for justice for myself and others. I'm Black history. My church highlighted me because of my fight for social justice. They see my resilience as a testimony to keeping the faith and pushing past my pain to find healing. I am honored to know that.

I cried when I first saw the video. This place that gave me so much honors me and honors the work that has been thrust upon me as a result of a horrific mistake. Yes, I know that God sent me to Progressive at just the right time, and I'm forever grateful. Reflecting on this realization helps me answer the question I kept in my mind for a while: *Where was God that night?*

Well, I now know God had not left me; God had actually prepared a way for me. I'm reminded again of Joseph from Genesis chapters 37–50. Joseph's entire life paved the way for his family to venture to Egypt at the right time. A famine was coming, and Joseph was in charge of the allocation of food.

We don't always like to think of the things we have to go through to get to our purpose. They are not always pretty. They are not always dreamy. Joseph dreamed of being in this position, but he just didn't know how he'd get there. And was he in for a bumpy ride. Yet God was faithful, and he really did become all he dreamed of. He just didn't have a clue as to how he'd get to his ultimate purpose. I think it's critical to note that Joseph's purpose wasn't really about him; it wasn't solely about him being the head of his brothers or the leader of the pack. No, it was about God's plan for him to help his family during a time of famine and hopelessness. God's plan was so much bigger than Joseph could grasp or imagine. It was so much more than just little Joseph leading his family.

I'm learning that God wanted more out of me. My life was not just for me. From the beginning, I was put here to help people. I know it. I see it in my grandmother. It was just a natural thing; we helped people. As a child, I never questioned it. I did what my grandmother told me to do, and I think serving just became a natural part of who I am. I'm sure that's a big part of the reason I went into social work. However, I had no idea that this is where I'd land—an advocate for people on a whole other level.

I never thought I'd be the one sitting across from lawmakers, standing before city councils, or meeting with the mayor to demand change. Yet here I am—speaking not just for myself but also for the countless Black and Brown people whose voices have been ignored, whose pain has been dismissed, and whose dignity has been stripped away by a system that was never built to protect them.

What I am doing now, thanks in large part to the support of Progressive, is more than activism. It is about fundamental human rights. It is about demanding that people be treated with dignity and respect—even as police officers do their jobs. It is about ensuring that our communities are not seen as war zones, that our homes are not treated like battlegrounds, and that our lives are not disposable.

We need reform. We need change. But more than that, we need to be seen, to be heard, and to be valued as human beings. I am here to make sure that happens—not just for myself but for every person who has ever felt powerless against this system.

I never would have imagined this would be my life and this would be my calling. But here I am. This calling found me as I pored through story after story, crying as I read through what occurred in the name of upholding the law. I cried and wept and relived my nightmare as I saw videos of what happened to children and innocent people. We can't go on like this. We need change.

I'm here to fight. I didn't choose this path; it chose me. And I'm here for it. I never saw myself in the space for advocacy. But now I have to continue to honor my grandmother and pick up the torch and continue to fight. That doesn't mean I feel good about the raid and what happened to me—how could I? But as things become clearer about my divinely ordered purpose, I can see God's hand working in this mess even when it doesn't feel good. With all I've learned from my research and incessant search for answers, with all of the families I've read about and even been able to meet and support after raids, I have the courage and strength to step forward. I feel a responsibility to speak up and change this system.

During my healing journey, my church became my comfort place, and it still is. What places have you found comfort in? Describe what you have felt—the smell, the colors, the sounds, etc.—surrounding your comfort place. How can you visit that place more frequently? Are there routines you can create that will offer structure and help you feel more in control or more at peace?

Advice from a Therapist

Alicia Troff-Meade, LCSW, discusses how finding a comfort place, like Anjanette Young's church, can assist in healing.

A comfort place quiets the vagus nerve, which is activated during trauma and reminds the traumatized person that there are indeed safe places out there where they can begin to build a sense of trust to heal. (The vagus nerve sends signals to the brain, heart, and digestive system.) Comfort places are often quiet places that emphasize calming and soothing activities, such as yoga centers, meditation centers, and spiritual centers that promote wholeness. These are good places to start, since trauma has an immediate and enduring effect on the body. Even when a traumatized individual thinks they're without bothersome thoughts, the body "stores" the trauma, which can confuse the individual (e.g., *Why am I having this reaction when I see myself as being fine?*).

7

SOCIAL WORKER TURNED ADVOCATE: HELPING OTHERS CAN HELP YOU HEAL

AS I'VE NOTED, it was a pretty natural decision for me to go into social work. I had seen my grandmother take care of people all of my life. She helped whoever was in need, including those in our family and those in our community. I was brought up to help my neighbor, doing whatever Ma told me to do—from delivering a meal to someone in need to stopping by to check on a sick neighbor. I had no clue this same gene would turn me into a vocal advocate, one who stands in front of lawmakers and fights for policy changes to help people who may not ever speak up for themselves.

What happened to me in my own apartment in 2019 opened my eyes wider to the injustices happening around us in the name of legal rights. I saw stories of raids where guns were drawn on kids. I saw for myself a gun drawn on my little Lexi. Of course, I was upset about what happened to me; it was unimaginable, and I will live with those vivid images for the rest of my life. Imagine what a child goes through when his surroundings are uprooted by officers in uniform. How could this be justice? How could this help alleviate crime? How is this serving and protecting us? It's not, and it's wrong. It's horribly tragic when innocent people are just trying to unwind from a day's work by watching TV and their doors burst open without warning and their lives are forever left with a traumatic imprint. It's insane that a zip code or neighborhood would be enough to make you invisible and a target all at once.

I have always believed that law enforcement should have the necessary tools and resources to fight crime effectively. However, that cannot come at the expense of people's rights and dignity—regardless of their skin color, economic status, or where they live. The ability to uphold public safety should never justify reckless policing, civil rights violations, or the dehumanization of innocent people.

After enduring my personal nightmare on February 21, 2019, I came to a painful realization: Equal protection under the law is not a reality for everyone, across much of this country and particularly in Chicago. The very system that is supposed to protect and serve all citizens fails to do so consistently, especially for marginalized communities. It became clear to me that in certain neighborhoods, police operate under a different set of rules—where assumptions, biases, and brute force take precedence over thorough investigation and due process. I was not treated as a law-abiding citizen, a professional, or even as a human being. Instead, I was treated as a suspect simply because of where I lived and the color of my skin.

This experience made me question everything I thought I knew about justice, fairness, and the role of law enforcement. If it could happen to me—a woman with no criminal record, minding her own business in her own home—how many others had suffered similar injustices without anyone ever hearing their stories? The fight against crime should never come at the cost of innocent people's safety, privacy, or fundamental rights. And until there is real accountability, the painful truth remains: justice in America is not applied equally.

As I've said before, my eyes were opened to the world of injustices taking place all around me. And while I knew injustice existed, having a personal experience like my raid made me even more sensitive and aware. I knew how damaging this process was and continued to be for me. As I read about other people's experiences, I just couldn't passively sit by. I became consumed with stories of injustice, desperate to understand why these violent police raids were happening with such frequency—and why Black and Brown people were disproportionately their victims. I needed to know: What was it about us? Why were so many Black women suffering at the hands of law enforcement? I read about Rekia Boyd and Aiyana Stanley-Jones, both murdered in 2012. I learned about Sandra Bland and Bettie Jones, taken from us in 2015. Atatiana Jefferson was killed in 2019, and then Breonna Taylor in March 2020. Even as I write this book, new names continue to be added to the tragic list—Nika Holbert, Sonya Massey—women whose lives were stolen by those who swore to protect and serve.

It was clear to me that this wasn't just a series of isolated incidents. This was systemic. It was deeply embedded in the way law enforcement views Black and Brown people, particularly women. But if this pattern was so evident, why weren't we stopping it? We live in an era where more people of color hold positions of political power and influence than ever before. Surely, they see what's happening. Surely, they recognize the harm being inflicted on our communities. And yet the violence continues. The injustices persist. So what will it take to end this?

I struggled with these questions around justice, feeling both enraged and helpless. How do we make them see our humanity? How do we force those in power to act, to dismantle a system that has repeatedly devalued our lives? These were not just philosophical musings—they were also survival questions. Because as long as these raids continue, as long as our deaths at the hands of law enforcement go unpunished, none of us are truly safe. We definitely need more than hashtags and momentary outrage. While those things can bring attention to the issues, we need someone fighting for policy change. We need people holding our lawmakers' feet to the fire and demanding change.

My New Role Emerges

These thoughts, realizations, and the constant uncovering of more stories of injustice led me to step into a role I now recognize as that of an advocate. I didn't anticipate how deeply the raid would alter my career trajectory. But as I delved deeper into systemic failures and the structural inequalities fueling them, I realized that advocacy was not just something I was doing—it was also something I had to do. It was no longer a choice; it was a calling. Without knowing it at the time, my journey had taken me through what I've described as a full-circle moment.

My background had always been in micro-level social work, where I worked directly with individuals, families, and small groups to help them navigate challenges, access resources, and improve their well-being. Micro-level social work focuses on one-on-one interactions—it's about meeting people where they are, listening to their struggles, and providing them with tools and support to overcome obstacles in their personal lives. Social workers at this level deal with the individual on the individual level and can be seen as the "first responders" to people's immediate needs. Clients may be individuals, families, or small groups. Micro social work is the work we do in social service agencies: we work directly with families and people experiencing some of the systemic issues of the day, and we provide counseling, intervention help, and anything else a family or individual may need to address personal challenges and improve their wellness. It's the work of my life. I spent my career here—making sure patients could get their medicine, making sure they took it, and making sure they had help in their homes. I helped mothers with no income get the resources they needed for their babies, such as diapers and other things we sometimes take for granted. I helped HIV patients and victims of domestic violence avoid homelessness by securing housing. This meant working directly with those in need of care. It could be frustrating some days—for instance, when I couldn't get the services right away, like when I had a mother in need of diapers and the resources would not be available for several days—but it was important work.

It is often behind-the-scenes work, and people never really understand its impact until they've needed the support and service of a micro-level social worker. To be successful in this work, you need to be someone who really cares and can cut through red tape to get people the help they desperately need. You need to be empathetic and see people not as numbers but as individuals who have needs—needs you can somehow meet to make their life more livable.

I had spent years dedicated to this work, believing in its power to create change on an individual level. And it does. When a person receives the right mental health support, when a struggling family gains access to safe housing, when a survivor of trauma is able to rebuild their life—these are victories that matter. They are real, tangible, and deeply personal. However, micro social work is often about addressing the symptoms, rather than the root causes, of larger systemic issues.

The more I researched and immersed myself in the realities of social injustice, the more I saw that many of the struggles individuals face are not just personal issues but also systemic failures. If communities of color are over-policed, if access to mental health resources is limited, if schools in marginalized neighborhoods lack funding, then no amount of one-on-one counseling or case management will ever be enough to truly solve the problem. I realized that real, lasting change requires macro-level social work, a broader approach that focuses on policy, legislation, and systemic transformation.

I'm typically a behind-the-scenes type of person; I enjoy one-on-one work with individuals. But ever since I conducted my research after the raid, I've known I can make a difference on a large scale. I'm lobbying for policy change. I tell my story for policy change. I tell the story of others for policy change. My voice can make a difference. My story can make a difference. This raid didn't happen in vain. My trauma is not in vain. I am using it to make things better, to bring awareness of the senselessness involved in some of these policies that let the police do things that are inhumane and hurtful. I especially work hard to protect children. A nine-year-old boy like my friend Peter Mendez should not have to live with the memories of police officers breaking into his home and pointing a gun at him and his younger brother. This was not necessary. This was not fighting crime.

In my new role in macro-level social work, I can advocate for the change that is needed in our system. I can't stand by and do nothing if I have the power to help others correct this wrong.

Of course, this conversation is complex and nuanced. I'm not saying police officers shouldn't ever raid homes. What I'm asking for and advocating for and shouting for and using every ounce of my work for is some reform. Let's be thoughtful and cautious and respectful of the innocent people hurt here. Police need to do their jobs. I'm fully supportive of police investigating crimes and bringing those who've done wrong to trial. It's important work. We need to abide by the laws to live in society. We need to hold those who break laws accountable. Absolutely. But when a system is so infiltrated with racism and disadvantages that it hurts poor children and interrupts the life of a woman who just went to work and church, that's not justice. That's not protecting and serving.

The macro-level work I'm doing now includes standing up in hearings and sharing my story so lawmakers can have a real-life picture of the damage our current system causes. I stand up and testify in both local and state committee meetings to share what happened to me and how it has eternally impacted my life so we can pass laws to prevent this type of damage from happening again.

In Chicago, five Black alderwomen—Maria Hadden, Sophia King, Leslie Hairston, Jeanette Taylor, and Stephanie Coleman—first introduced the Anjanette Young Ordinance in 2021. We asked for tighter guidelines to protect residents during these raids, but the ordinance died in committee.

But we're not giving up. We are fighters, and I'm even more charged up to right some wrongs. I have helped craft laws around search warrant regulations as well as no-knock warrants. I'd ideally like to see the police give people time—even just thirty seconds—to answer their door when a search warrant is being served before the officers proceed to break in. Let people at least be dressed and open the door as opposed to police officers immediately knocking it down and damaging property. (By the way, my apartment complex tried to charge me for repairing my door when those officers broke it. Had I not had such an excellent attorney who fought that charge, I'd be left with a bill for the damage. Where is the justice in that? What happens when people do not have stellar attorneys and support from their church? Do they just pay the bill? Do they fight with their apartment complex?) Injustice reaps even more injustice, and the only ones getting hurt are those who are voiceless or poor or without the adequate resources. The ordinance introduced in Chicago City Council also asked for protection of children by prohibiting officers from pointing guns at them during these raids.

In my new advocacy role, I show up for others in court so they know there is someone who understands a part of their story. I speak for the babies and the children who will live with those internal scars forever as their home was entered in the dark of the night and taken over by officers with guns drawn. I share my story for impact and influence. I tell of what happened to me so it might not happen to another. I allow the body cam video of February 21, 2019, to be played showing me as I stand in my home screaming for the police officers to stop or to let me know what's happening, telling them they have the wrong place, so others won't have to go through that. I use my voice as a woman standing naked in her own home so we can make changes on a systemic level. The micro level, the individual, is being severely and negatively affected by the system. I am now working on a macro level to change the system so individuals will have safer, better lives.

Macro social work is about changing the structures that create and sustain inequality. It's about addressing the policies that allow injustices—like the one I personally experienced—to happen in the first place. It's about holding institutions accountable and ensuring that marginalized voices are not just heard but also valued in decision-making spaces. Shifting into macro social work has meant stepping outside the intimate, direct work I had been doing for years and instead engaging in advocacy, policy reform, and large-scale social change. It means attending meetings with lawmakers, pushing for police accountability measures, speaking at public forums, and working alongside other advocates/activists and professionals to demand systemic reform.

This transition has not been easy. There's a certain comfort in working at the micro level because you can see the direct impact of your efforts. You witness the progress, however small, in the lives of those you help. Macro work, on the other hand, is a long game. Policy changes can take years, sometimes decades, to materialize. The work is often frustrating and slow-moving. But the impact, when successful, is far-reaching—it has the power to reshape entire communities and generations to come.

I now understand that both micro and macro social work are necessary. One cannot exist without the other. We need professionals in schools, hospitals, and crisis centers supporting individuals through their struggles, but we also need people working behind the scenes to change the laws and policies that make those struggles so common in the first place.

What happened to me forced me to see the limitations of micro social work alone. My advocacy was born from necessity, but it has since evolved into purpose. I am no longer just working to help individuals recover from trauma—I am also fighting to prevent the trauma from happening in the first place.

And for that reason, I'm not turning back.

I believe there's a lot of work to be done around police training, especially when dealing with people in the Black and Brown communities. There is a culture of the police just not caring about this community and not using the same type of care and sensitivity when dealing with us. This lack of sensitivity was on full display in my apartment that night. It's the reason I agreed to allow the world to see the body cam video, to see the forty minutes of my screeching pleas telling them they had the wrong person, they had the wrong place. Yet the officers ignored me. They pushed me to the side and ran through my place without regard to my screams, my nakedness, or even due process within the system. They didn't care. They went on a tip to find a gun, and they did not do the work to verify it. Why? Why wouldn't they care about me as a human being?

It is my job now to change the culture of not caring and push for everyone to be treated as a human with dignity, even as police officers do the work to protect us and find those who have broken the law. What my grandmother showed me about standing up for what is right—regardless of whom you have to stand up to—has rubbed off on me. When I sat in the aftermath of this tragedy and waited long hours, days, and months for justice, I knew I had to keep fighting. My grandmother wouldn't have stood for anything else. Even through her death and grave, I felt a sense of responsibility to fix this, to do something. I had to speak up.

As I've said before, my first demand was that all twelve officers involved in the raid be fired. It seemed like the most basic form of justice. They had violated my rights, humiliated me, and turned my life upside down—all based on an unreliable tip. But when I brought this up to Keenan, he quickly let me know that's not how the system worked. I struggled to grasp why there was so little accountability in law enforcement. In my field, if I made a critical mistake, there would be consequences. If a doctor makes a life-threatening error, they can be sued for malpractice and potentially lose their license. If a social worker mishandles a case and causes harm, they can be fired or have their license revoked. Even teachers, lawyers, and business professionals are held to professional standards that demand accountability. But for some reason, police officers—who literally have the power to take lives—are shielded from the kind of repercussions that apply to almost every other profession.

I couldn't understand how these officers had faced no disciplinary action for what they did to me. They didn't do due diligence. They conducted no surveillance, no verification, no background checks before storming into my home. Instead, they acted on a tip from a young man trying to cut a deal—someone who had every reason to lie in order to protect himself. And yet, when it came down to it, I was the one left to suffer the consequences of their negligence. The reason for this lack of accountability? Qualified immunity.

Qualified immunity is a legal doctrine that protects police officers and other government officials from being sued for violating someone's constitutional rights—unless it can be proven that they violated "clearly established law." Essentially, unless there is a nearly identical past case that explicitly deems the officer's actions unlawful, they are shielded from civil lawsuits. This makes it nearly impossible for victims of police misconduct to get justice in court. Even in cases where officers act recklessly, they are rarely held personally liable for the harm they cause. This system creates an environment where officers feel emboldened to act without fear of repercussions. If they don't face consequences for their mistakes—if they aren't held accountable for their actions—then what incentive do they have to change? What stops them from continuing to recklessly destroy lives like they did mine?

Understanding this made me even angrier. How could we expect change when the system was designed to protect the people causing harm? I was living proof that police misconduct wasn't just something that happened in news headlines—it was real, it was personal, and it was devastating. As Keenan says, they came into my apartment as if it was Beirut or Baghdad or the center of a war zone and treated me like a criminal based on just a small tip from another person caught up in criminal charges. Yet the system that allowed it to happen was still standing, untouched. That had to change.

In civil suits like mine, some people may focus on the money. Ultimately, I settled with the city for $2.9 million for this case, but as I often say, if I could have gotten those officers fired, I would have been happy with no money. When I told my pastor I was considering settling at this point, he was grateful. He agreed with my choice. Pastor Charlie said, "No amount of money would fully compensate for or erase what happened to you." He continued, "If you keep pushing for the city to do more when they aren't willing to, you're going to cause more harm to yourself." He says he wanted me to pick up and move forward with my life, which shows what a great pastor he is; he was more worried about my well-being than anything else. He recalls, "We wanted her [Anjanette] to be healthy, and I believed that healing from God would give her the strength she needed, not money."

He was absolutely right, and my fight was not to get a cash payout. My fight was—and still is—to bring justice, especially to people who do not have a voice, people who do not have influence in city hall or in the state legislature.

Through my painful experience, I have been thrust into a battle that is much bigger than myself—a battle against a broken system that continues to violate, dehumanize, and strip away the dignity of so many Black and Brown people. With my platform, I now have an opportunity to amplify this problem on a national scale. I have spoken with Joy Reid and Gayle King. I have shared my truth with people who have the power to influence change. My voice has reached places I never imagined. And yet this fight is not just about me. It is also about every person who has suffered injustice at the hands of law enforcement.

When I think about my journey, I cannot help but think about all the other Black women in Chicago and around the country who lost their lives. God covered me and gave me a testimony, and I realized that my voice mattered—not just in telling my own story but also in demanding systemic change. This is what emerging from trauma with purpose looks like for me.

I have worked with numerous legislators at both the city and state levels to push for policies that hold police accountable for their interactions with Black and Brown communities. However, progress on the city level has been frustratingly slow. As I write this, it has been four years since I first introduced the Anjanette Young Ordinance to the Chicago City Council; however, city officials have continuously failed to take the necessary steps to pass it into law. Despite countless meetings, advocacy efforts, and community support, there has been a clear lack of political will to enact real change.

Recognizing these roadblocks, I shifted to plan B—taking the fight to the state level. My goal has been to pass legislation in Illinois that would not only force Chicago to adopt meaningful reforms but also create statewide policies that protect residents from unjust police practices. By pushing for change on a broader scale, we can ensure that every city, every town, and every community in Illinois is held to the same standard of accountability. While the city has dragged its feet, momentum at the state level has been stronger. Working with state lawmakers, I have fought to advance policies that would establish stricter guidelines for police conduct, ensure better oversight of search warrants, and provide real consequences for officers who violate people's rights. This work is far from over, but I remain committed to seeing it through. If the city refuses to act, the state will force their hand. Change is coming—one way or another.

My fight for justice is more than just telling our stories. It's about changing the laws that allow these injustices to continue. My fight is our fight; it is for every person who has ever been brutalized, violated, or dehumanized by the system. The trauma we experienced—police storming into our homes, violating our dignity, leaving us with lasting wounds—should never happen again. That is why, as I am writing this book, Illinois House Bill 1611 (HB1611) has been introduced and passed committee, which is the first of many steps to get this bill signed into law. We have more people of color in political office than ever before. We have seen symbolic progress—police reform bills, diversity initiatives—but what has truly changed? Why are we still having the same conversations, still fighting the same battles, still watching Black and Brown people be brutalized by a system that claims to serve and protect them?

This Is Bigger than Me

I know that my trauma will always be a part of me. I will never forget what it felt like to stand in my own home, naked and terrified, as officers pointed guns at me. I will never forget the powerlessness, the rage, the humiliation. But I have turned my pain into purpose.

Every time I speak out, every time I share my story, and every time I push for policy change, I am reclaiming my power. My experience will not be reduced to just another statistic. I refuse to be a passive victim, silenced by trauma or overshadowed by bureaucracy. Instead, I have chosen to stand in my truth, to make sure my story is heard, and to fight for a future where no one else has to endure what I did.

When the video of my wrongful raid was released, I knew my first interview would be more than just a moment to tell my side of the story—it would also be a statement. That day, I wore a T-shirt I had designed myself. It bore the face of Breonna Taylor, a young Black woman who, like me, had suffered the horror of a no-knock raid. Above her image were the words I AM HER.

Wearing that shirt was my way of honoring Breonna's life while sharing my own story. It was a declaration that what happened to Breonna, what happened to me, and what has happened to so many Black and Brown people across this country is part of the same devastating reality. I wanted the world to understand that our stories are connected, that our pain is collective, and that our fight for justice is far from over.

Over time, that T-shirt became more than just a piece of clothing. It became a vision, a mission, and ultimately, the foundation for something bigger than myself—the I AM HER Foundation. What began as a personal tribute evolved into an organization dedicated to supporting others who have experienced trauma, wrongful police violence, and systemic injustice.

When I received my settlement, I understood that no amount of money could ever erase what I had endured. The fear, the humiliation, the violation of my most sacred space—none of it could be undone with a check. But I also knew that I had a choice: to let that pain consume me or to transform it into something meaningful.

I chose the latter.

Through the I AM HER Foundation, I have been further able to turn my pain into purpose. I have found ways to support survivors, to amplify their voices, and to demand real change. My journey has shown me that healing isn't just about moving on, it's about moving forward with intention. Whether it's a result of domestic violence, sexual abuse, wrongful police raids, or the everyday violence that plagues our communities, trauma leaves wounds that are often unseen but deeply felt.

This foundation is my way of saying, *I see you. I hear you. You are not alone.* It's a space for survivors to find resources, advocacy, and, most important, hope. I want women and girls to know that their pain does not define them—their strength, their resilience, and their ability to rise again does.

Through this work, I am not just honoring my own journey through trauma—I am also standing in solidarity with every woman who has ever felt unheard, unseen, and unprotected. We are in this together. This is not just about me or my personal issue, it's about creating a system where every person, regardless of their race or zip code, is treated with dignity and respect. I will continue to fight, to push, and to demand action. Because justice delayed is justice denied.

Don't get me wrong, not everyone who experiences trauma and pushes past their pain will have a national platform; nor will body cam footage be shown forever when their name is googled. Trust me, it can be a blessing to be able to live a private life, one hopefully filled with private healing. But some healing does take place in public and within community.

As Camille Quinn says about healing in community, "You can decide how you become the fullest person you're supposed to be; it's up to you and how you fortify yourself and what you do to co-create. . . . Many do it in community with sorors (sorority sisters), friends, church members, or immediate families . . . healing is finding ways to make overall quality of life fulfilling and enjoyable; you want to do more, give more, be more . . . and you can't do that in a space of deprivation."

Finding my voice and standing up for others has been a big part of my healing journey. At times, uncovering all these other cases—realizing more and more how devalued our people are—has been disheartening and tough to swallow. But knowing that I can do something, knowing that I am doing something—something I would not have even thought to work toward or fight for before February 21, 2019—makes my healing more tangible and purposeful. I know that what happened to me that night was not in vain. Even though it was ruthless and cold and careless and reckless and a total disregard for me as a person, the process, the pain, and the healing are being put to some good use. For that, I'm proud. For that, I'm grateful. For that, I not only want to work to enact change around police treatment of Black and Brown citizens, but as a social worker with a heart for helping people heal, I also want to tell women who have been traumatized that there is hope. There is healing. It is available. I'm a witness.

Where Was God?

My faith tells me this journey has been orchestrated by God. My faith reminds me that while I didn't sense God's presence that night and my early days were filled with lots of questions, I now see God's hand all over this ordeal. "You intended to harm me, but God intended it for good to accomplish what is now being done, the saving of many lives." This comes from Genesis 50:20. It's what Joseph said to his brothers when he was helping save his family from famine. He realized his entire life had been preparing him for such a pivotal moment—God used the evil he experienced to accomplish good. Back when he was going through his many ordeals, he'd had no idea. He didn't know what God would do, but he kept trusting and living for God.

That's who I desire to be. I kept doing what I thought I was supposed to do in life. Even when I stumbled or got lost, I used my faith in God as a compass to get back on a path. I was knocked off-kilter and off my square that night in 2019. I questioned God. I wondered why and how this happened to me—the woman who was just working and going to church and trying to help somebody along the way. But now I see it. I see it much more clearly. God turned this awful situation into my purpose.

That's a beautiful thing about purpose and God's orchestration of it. It's not just about me. This is not Anjanette Young's story. This is much bigger than me. It's much greater than a little social work consulting business. This is about restoring dignity to God's people: the ones we consider the least of these; the ones who may not be able to meet with legislators and share their own stories. This is why I'm here. Just as Joseph was the conduit to save his family from famine, I see my purpose as being a conduit to save people from mistreatment and malicious and reckless policies that can leave their life in pieces. I'm here to share how trauma doesn't have to be the place you stay.

As Camille Quinn says, "I am not my trauma; trauma is what happened to me, but that's not who I am." Those working with people who have experienced trauma need to remember this and act accordingly. Those who have experienced trauma need to also look beyond the traumatic event and embrace the fact that they are more than that experience. They are not the bad thing that happened to them. "The only way we can heal is to come to grips with all of it and to love ourselves anyway. Trauma is one part. We have a whole bunch of parts."

Who do you say you are? Describe yourself—including the parts you see as good and positive as well as other parts. How can you reintroduce yourself to embrace the statement "you are not your trauma"? Who are you?

Advice from My Own Journal on Healing —Anjanette Young

My own healing journey has revealed a deep truth: things will *not* return to their original version.

Traumatic experiences shake up the world as you once knew it, but healing will allow you to lean into the recovery process and the newness that emerges. You will *not* adjust easily to adversity or change. But over time, you will find your individual pace for resiliency, as it looks different for everyone. Be patient with yourself. Give yourself big doses of grace.

Healing is not about bouncing back unchanged or moving through adversity with ease. It is about finding a new way to navigate the world, one that honors your unique process and the growth that emerges from challenges.

8

I AM A TESTIMONY

SOME MOMENTS ON your healing journey will seem mundane, or even like nothing is happening. Others will feel like setbacks, like when you wake up in a moment of panic—recalling the abuse, the wrong, the hurt, and pain—and forget where you are and just how far you've come. There are also some aha moments when you feel the healing, you see the healing, you recognize the growth—tangible times when you have to stop and embrace what has occurred. I hope and pray you keep moving when you experience any or all of these moments.

In the mundane moments, remind yourself of just how far you've come. Often, things feel like they are not moving or changing. In the midst of the pandemic, I felt like this when the courts were closed and my case against the City of Chicago was at a standstill. Such moments can leave you wondering how everyone around you is able to move on when you cannot. Your traumatic experience is your constant companion, a nagging and hurtful sidekick. But remind yourself that you will not be stuck here forever.

Healing from trauma is not a linear process—it's a winding journey filled with peaks of progress, valleys of pain, and long stretches where simply putting one foot in front of the other feels like an act of defiance. For me, on some days healing feels tangible, like I am reclaiming my power and moving forward with purpose. Other days, it feels like I am barely holding on, just trying to make it through the next moment. But what I've come to understand is that healing isn't measured by how fast or how far I go—it's in the simple act of continuing.

There is strength in survival, even when it doesn't feel like progress. There is power in choosing to wake up and face the world despite the weight of past wounds. I've learned that healing isn't always about grand gestures or transformative moments, it's about the quiet victories. Healing is taking deep breaths when anxiety rises, allowing myself to feel without shame, and embracing the journey with all its imperfections.

Through this process, I've discovered resilience I never knew I had. I've found purpose in my pain and strength in my scars. I've come to accept that healing is not about forgetting what happened but about refusing to let it define me. No matter how slow the progress, every step forward is a testament to my survival, my strength, and my unwavering determination to keep going.

When you've been deeply hurt, the world doesn't stop to give you time to heal. You still have to wake up, go to work, pay the bills, and take care of daily responsibilities. But in those moments—whether it's making your morning coffee, taking a walk, or even just getting through a work meeting—you are proving to yourself that you are still here. That you are still standing.

My advice? Give yourself grace. Healing doesn't mean forgetting. It doesn't mean the pain disappears overnight—if it disappears at all. But it does mean allowing yourself to move through life at your own pace. Find joy in small things, lean on the people who uplift you, and don't be afraid to ask for help. As Dr. Wilborn notes, "It is okay to get support when you're not okay. Sometimes you will be able to manage distress and difficulties on your own. If what you are doing is working, then keep doing it. However, if what you are doing does not work or you need someone to support you . . . that is okay too."

Some days, you'll feel strong. Other days, you'll feel like you're barely holding on. Both are OK. In chapter 1, we said it's OK not to be OK. That was so liberating for me as I fought hard to move on and get back to myself. I had to realize that some days I just was not OK. Being strong or barely holding on—both are part of healing. What matters is that you keep going, because every step, no matter how small, is a victory. You are not your trauma. You are your resilience.

And when those awful flashbacks try to paralyze you, it's totally OK to sit with the emotions, the memories, the pain. It's also what Alicia said in chapter 1. Sitting with emotions helps you identify what is occurring, especially when you use a practice like mindfulness. Alicia also said to observe that emotion, not judge it. After all, as Alicia stressed, "It is only when you understand what is happening to you emotionally that you can begin to choose what you want and set a plan to move forward." So even when those flashbacks occur and stir up emotions inside of you, it's not just pain in vain. It can be used to help you move forward. I've learned not to run away from my flashback moments. They too can serve a purpose.

Hands down, my favorite moments on this journey are now what I and Oprah call aha moments. As mentioned earlier, these are times when you get a clearer glimpse of your healing and perhaps even your purpose. An aha moment is a moment to celebrate this journey. Although I would not have chosen the trauma that happened to me when the police raided my apartment, looking for some unknown person who possessed a gun, I have moments when I can see God's amazing hand all over this incident, all over me, and all over my life. It is in these aha moments that I can celebrate and realize this journey is not by happenstance.

I'd like to share one of my aha moments and how it has continued to carry me through some mundane moments and seemingly setback moments.

One Sunday, a few years after the raid and a few years into this healing journey, as I made my way to my beloved church where I stood guard welcoming people into worship service, I met an aha moment. I can't fully remember how I was feeling that day, but I think the day was pretty normal. I showed up because that's what I do. I was taught to be faithful and to be a woman of my word. If I was scheduled to serve, I served, regardless of how I felt or the emotions that were pulling at me. If it was Sunday, I was at my post with a smile on my face, genuinely happy to welcome worshipers to Progressive. Serving has been one of my love languages and one of the ways I thank God as well as connect to the beautiful memory of my grandmother. So I showed up to serve. But I would have never guessed my aha moment would be embodied by a young (to me) sister dressed beautifully and wearing noticeably high-heeled shoes. She was the guest preacher for the day's service.

I thank God that my pastor often brings in powerhouse preachers whom he has met in his travels and ministry. He is a dynamic preacher and pastor himself, so he shares his pulpit with like-minded people. This day, this young, beautiful sister caught my attention. Her physical presence, as striking as it was, was only surface for me. What she said—in her high-pitched voice with a sort of Southern or Texas twang—has stayed with me for many years. It changed my life. It changed my perspective of what happened to me.

Dr. Brianna Parker, our guest preacher, spoke about the text of 2 Kings 8:1–6. I'll try to do her sermon justice by retelling some of it here, but watching her deliver the same sermon on YouTube (https://www.youtube.com/watch?v=b8oPpvEt8Kk) will give a more complete picture of what she said and how she presented the word of God in a way that gave me an aha moment.

The message was titled "Interest on Investment." It would be helpful to understand the background story too. For those who may not be familiar with this story, the setup can be found in 2 Kings 4:8–37. The Old Testament prophet Elisha met a woman from Shunem (she is also called a Shunammite) who invited him to stay at her home—she was showing hospitality and desiring to help the man of God. She was also considered wealthy and had the means to help. As a way of repaying her, the prophet asked what he could do for her. She told Elisha she had enough—after all, she was "well-to-do," as 2 Kings 4:8 describes her. But then Elisha's servant intervened and told the prophet the woman didn't have a son and her husband was old. So Elisha proclaimed that the woman would have a son within a year. And what the prophet said actually did occur. The woman gave birth to a son later that year.

But the story doesn't end there. When the Shunammite woman's child grew a little older, he died unexpectantly after complaining of a headache. When the boy died, the Shunammite woman went to summon Elisha. She reminded Elisha that she hadn't even asked for the child! "Did I ask you for a son, my lord?" she said. "Didn't I tell you, 'Don't raise my hopes'?" (2 Kings 4:28). The woman felt as if the child was a bonus, something added to her life when she hadn't even asked for a child. She had buried that desire deep inside of her, yet through the intervention of the servant, Elisha had pronounced that she would have the child. How do you deal with an unrequested gift that has been unexpectantly snatched away? How do you live when your life seems fine and then it is interrupted and turned upside down?

I identified with this woman written about thousands of years ago in the Old Testament of the Bible. My culture and my time are drastically different than hers, but as Dr. Parker preached, this Shunammite woman became alive to me. I leaned in a bit closer and took even more note of Dr. Parker's words.

So disappointed, mad, and feisty, this woman demanded that Elisha, the prophet, come back to her home to see about her child, who was dead. Elisha eventually went to the woman's home to bring the boy back to life. As noted in 2 Kings 4:33–37:

> 33 He [Elisha] went in, shut the door on the two of
> them and prayed to the Lord. 34 Then he got on the
> bed and lay on the boy, mouth to mouth, eyes to eyes,
> hands to hands. As he stretched himself out on him,
> the boy's body grew warm. 35 Elisha turned away and
> walked back and forth in the room and then got on

> the bed and stretched out on him once more. The boy
> sneezed seven times and opened his eyes.
> [36] Elisha summoned Gehazi [his servant] and said,
> "Call the Shunammite." And he did. When she came,
> he said, "Take your son." [37] She came in, fell at his
> feet and bowed to the ground. Then she took her
> son and went out.

The book of 2 Kings goes on to tell a few other stories before it returns to the Shunammite woman in chapter 8, which is where Dr. Parker picked up her sermon.

Apparently, the prophet told the woman to leave her land, because there would be a famine for seven years. She did as she was told, and she was protected. But when the seven years were over, she returned to her hometown and asked for her land. She had to appeal to the king; the king asked Gehazi (the servant) to share some of the things Elisha had done in the land. The servant pointed to the Shunammite woman and said that she could tell the king and show him what Elisha did. The king turned to the woman and asked her what happened.

This is the part I resonate with and continue to think about several years later. Dr. Parker said the Shunammite "woman walked in with a testimony." She was called to the king to share just what Elisha had done—the miracle of having a child when she didn't have one and then the miracle of resurrecting that child.

However, Dr. Parker said, "the woman not only walked in with a testimony, she was a testimony." The fact that the lady was present meant she could show the king what happened; she could give her testimony. Dr. Parker said sometimes our mere presence is a testimony; it reminds others of just what we've been through. It reminds others of just how far God has indeed brought us.

The reminder that my story is serving as a testimony hit me. In going public just to get the attention of the police department and get a portion of some justice, I had to show people the video that was extremely personal and hurting. I had to let the world see me inside my own apartment, with a blanket draped over my naked body, screaming and yelling that the police had the wrong place. I bared it all, but now I was a testimony. My just showing up at this church or really any place is a reminder of what God has done. When I show up healed, I am a reminder of my testimony. I'm a reminder of all I've been through and that I'm still here. My presence is a testimony.

As Dr. Parker put it, "Somebody needs your testimony, and I need you present for something else. . . . When God keeps you for something, it's so you can tell the story." She emphasized the importance of telling your own story, saying that other people would "report it [what you've been through] as the facts of an interesting story, although you lived it as a nightmare." That was me. That was my story. I had lived through a nightmare.

Dr. Parker was speaking to the entire congregation, yet it felt as if she was speaking directly to me and my situation. She shared stories of people enduring hardship and emerging with a powerful testimony. That was me. People saw the press conferences, the interviews, the public statements—but they didn't see the lonely nights, the weight of my nightmare, or the struggle it took to reach a place where I could even speak about this injustice.

Dr. Parker's words resonated deeply. The same space the Shunammite woman prepared for Elisha—a simple bed—became the very place where her miracle occurred; Elisha healed her son and brought him back to life on that same bed. "The place you make for healing," she said, "might be the same place where your miracle happens. If you don't create space for someone else's healing, their productivity, maybe that space won't be available for your own miracle. Sometimes we think we're planting for others, but we're actually planting for our own harvest."

That was exactly what I was doing. My testimony had become a space for others to heal, for voices to be heard, and for justice to be pursued. I wasn't just telling my story—I was living it, embodying it. I walked in as a testimony, and I walked with a testimony. Like the Shunammite woman, my very presence bore witness to the power of resilience.

Dr. Parker declared, "Your presence alone is a testimony." And I knew it was true. Showing up—at church, at work, in life—was proof of my survival. Despite what I had been through, I was still standing. I wanted people to see my journey and believe that they, too, could survive, heal, and fight for justice.

"God, I see what You've done for others, and I know You can do it for me." That is my prayer. My life itself is a testimony. My story shows that healing is possible even after the darkest of nights. It proves that pain can be transformed into purpose, even a purpose we never anticipated.

Because of what I've been through, I am a testimony. My presence is a reminder of the power of healing, the strength of endurance, and the beauty of finding meaning beyond the pain. And the same can be true of you.

Dr. Parker goes on to say our testimony is a ticket to greater, which is the theme of interest on investment. When we share what has happened, it can point people to their own healing. When this woman told her story, the king restored whatever she had. The Shunammite woman got her land back—with interest—because of her testimony.

Dr. Parker encouraged us to be OK with sharing the truth of where we've been. Her message clicked for me. Someone needs to see my testimony. I went months without sharing what happened. But then I was forced to speak up and bring my story to CBS Chicago because I needed the video footage released; we needed to push the city's hand. I became a public figure, not because I wanted to but because I had to.

A well-known Scripture that many Christians quote really does sum things up beautifully and accurately: "And we know that in all things God works for the good of those who love him, who have been called according to his purpose" (Romans 8:28).

Wow! God worked things together for my good, and I was realizing it like never before.

What practices inspire you on your healing journey? (For me, it is attending church and hearing sermons like Dr. Brianna Parker's.) How can you commit to finding practices to assist you in your journey as you look for your purpose to emerge?

Recording Your Thoughts and Feelings

Another practice that has been of help to me is keeping a journal. It's not something I had consistently done before; writing down my thoughts was never a daily practice for me. But after the raid on my home, everything changed. Sleep became elusive—my mind a constant whirlwind of fear, anger, and unanswered questions. The nights felt endless, filled with replayed memories and emotions I couldn't escape.

In those restless hours, I found myself reaching for my phone, opening the Notepad app, and pouring my thoughts onto the screen. It wasn't about crafting perfect sentences or organizing my feelings in a coherent way. It was simply an attempt to unload the weight of my thoughts, to release them from my mind and make space for even a moment of peace. Writing became a desperate search for clarity, a way to process the trauma that refused to let me rest.

Looking back, those late-night reflections were more than just scattered words on a screen. They were my way of reclaiming control, of giving myself permission to acknowledge my pain rather than suppress it. Though I didn't realize it at the time, those journal entries became part of my healing—a quiet, personal act of survival in the midst of chaos. So here I share the process I went through to write a particular journal entry, which is included at the end of this section. I share this process in hopes that it can offer a sense of hope that you too can find a path forward from the staggering mundane moments. I hope you can use my thinking to put your own process into action as you continue to journey toward healing.

The week I wrote the following reflection had been particularly difficult—though, in truth, I can't recall exactly what had happened. Trauma has a way of blurring time, making bad days blend into one another. But I remember the weight of it. I remember finding myself stuck in a loop, replaying my last therapy session with Alicia over and over in my mind. She had challenged me in a way I wasn't expecting, asking me why I don't feel worthy.

Her question lingered long after our session ended. I had shared with her how uncomfortable it made me when people from the public called me their hero. It felt strange, almost unsettling, to be seen that way—to be placed on a pedestal for simply surviving something I still didn't fully understand. How could I be a hero for enduring a nightmare I never asked for? For making it through a trauma that, even now, still weighed on me in ways I couldn't always put into words? Alicia's words forced me to confront something deeper—something I had avoided for so long. *Why did I struggle with feeling worthy of the praise, the recognition, the acknowledgment of my own strength? Why did surviving feel like something I had to downplay rather than own?*

Then my mind went to me sitting in church back in early November 2021, when there was a guest speaker, Pastor F. Bruce Williams from Louisville, Kentucky. He was visiting as our senior pastor was taking a needed break from his Sunday-morning preaching duties. Pastor Williams is a tall, dark-skinned African American man whose presence cannot be missed as he towers over the podium. This particular Sunday was no different. At my church, Progressive Baptist, there were beautiful yellow, white, and green flower bouquets that decorated the pulpit. The sanctuary was about three-fourths full and everyone was attentive, waiting to hear an amazing word from God from our guest speaker.

It was the end of his very riveting message that struck me as being so powerful. He asked the question: Do you know who you are? I often reflect on that question as I listen to others describe me as strong, courageous, and inspiring because of how I have chosen to present myself after being traumatized, humiliated, and ignored by a Chicago Police Department raid team.

All I could see in myself was hurt, pain, weakness, and many nights of silent tears. Silent because on that awful night I cried out over forty times with tears streaming down my face, "You have the wrong place!" but no one listened. I had silent tears. Silent because I could not feel God's presence nor understand how He could let this happen to me! Silent tears.

I've spent a great deal of time with my therapist unpacking why I didn't feel good about others mentioning these positive attributes. Alicia's exact words to me were: "Why do you hide in the shadows of unworthiness?"

I will be honest, I was taken aback at the way she described it. I left that particular session downright angry! How dare she imply that I struggle with self-worth? I know who I am and what I bring to the table!

At least that's what I heard. I never thought of myself that way, but I was committed to the therapeutic process, so I spent the next several days in self-reflection and prayer. I needed to know what Alicia was seeing that made her take me down this road. Well, without sharing all the personal details, I can say it was a well-spent journey to learn that there was a part of me who unknowingly lived in the shadow of unworthiness because I didn't have a full understanding of who I was! (Side note: It's totally OK to disagree with statements your therapist makes; actually, it is also healthy. Therapists are not the end-all and be-all; they are not God. They do not know everything about you. They are only meant to guide you to come up with the answers yourself.)

Reflecting on the powerful sermon from Pastor Williams, I realized something I hadn't fully grasped before: I had been losing myself in the mundane, consumed by the weight of trauma. There was so much emotional heaviness surrounding me that I had become absorbed in the day-to-day struggle of just trying to keep moving forward. Pastor Williams's words shed light on the fact that when we face deep pain, especially trauma, we often find ourselves stuck in negative thought patterns. The daily grind can feel like an endless loop, and sometimes, in our efforts to just survive, we forget who we are or lose sight of ourselves along the way.

It was an eye-opening realization, because it wasn't something I was doing intentionally, and it wasn't a reflection of weakness. It wasn't my fault that I'd been submerged in the struggle. This was simply the reality of healing and living through trauma. It's something many of us go through, even though we don't always have the words to explain it. Pastor Williams's words were a reminder that it's OK to feel lost in the midst of our healing. It doesn't make us weak; it makes us human. Sometimes, it just is—part of the journey of reclaiming ourselves amid the pain.

As I reflected on this, I realized that healing doesn't always look like moving forward with strength and clarity. Sometimes, it looks like being gentle with ourselves through the quiet, uncertain moments. We're allowed to get lost. The important part is that we find our way back. So, as I prayed about this reflection Alicia forced me to think about, I wrote in my journal what I believe is how *God* sees me. It was an important takeaway for that night, and I often go back to my journal entry to build myself up during the hard moments. I hope that you can use it the same way, or better yet you can write your own reflection on how you imagine God sees you.

I AM HER
I am an African American woman, descendant of slaves, follower of Christ, Lucendia's grandbaby, social worker extraordinaire, a fighter for justice, mother of one, friend and family member of many.

All of who I am has been shaped and molded by the red clay dirt of the Mississippi Delta, and the spiritual breath of life from God which guides my moral compass.

I have always felt strongly that on that Thursday night, February 21, 2019, my tears and excruciating cries were silenced because no one would listen to me as I continued to tell them that they had the wrong place. No one responded to me when I asked to be allowed to put clothing on! It was the one thing that stood out the most: Why did they ignore me?

As I continue to reflect and seek God for my healing, I am learning that my cries and tears were silenced before I ever took my first breath! I was born into an ancestry where the cries of my people were ignored (slavery). There are times recorded in the Bible where the cries of the Israelites were met with silence. For a period of time God was not on the scene; it could be implied for a moment of time he ignored them.

So no wonder, li'l ol' me, the person who proudly owns that my mere being is rooted in God and my Mississippi heritage; me who loves to say, "I am just a little country girl from Mississippi whose grandmother introduced her to Jesus and taught her how to love others" was used and trusted by God on February 21, 2019, to lead such a tremendous battle against an unjust system.

There lies the answer to the question "God, why me?" Why did I have this experience of being ignored, humiliated, and have my tears fall silent to the twelve men who stood in front of my naked body? My silent tears are a part of a larger plan, which will have a loud thunderous outcome!

Who is Anjanette Young? She is a woman of God who has learned to see all of life's experiences through a spiritual lens of knowing that "all things work together for the good of those who love God and are called according to his purpose!" (Romans 8:28)

9

ON SELF-CARE

AS A CLINICIAN, I've had the opportunity to attend several professional development trainings focused on self-care. One of the key takeaways from these sessions is that "self-care is not a buzzword." It is an essential practice for mental health, well-being, and overall life satisfaction, particularly in fields where emotional and physical strain are common, such as social work, healthcare, and education.

Self-care isn't just about spa days or taking a break from work. It's a holistic, intentional approach to maintaining a healthy balance between mind, body, and spirit. Research shows that engaging in self-care practices can have profound benefits for both personal and professional growth. For example, according to the American Psychological Association, people who engage in self-care regularly experience lower levels of stress and higher levels of emotional well-being. They also report better relationships with others and improved productivity at work. Self-care has been linked to better physical health as well, including lower blood pressure, improved immune function, and a reduction in chronic conditions like anxiety and depression.

As someone who works in a profession centered around helping others, I understand the challenges of balancing the demands of the job with personal well-being. Clinicians, in particular, often experience burnout due to the emotionally taxing nature of the work. Studies show that over 50 percent of social workers and healthcare providers report feeling burned out at some point in their careers. This is why self-care is crucial—it helps to replenish our energy so we can continue to serve others effectively.

Ultimately, self-care is not an indulgence, it is a necessity. It is a practice that must be integrated into our daily lives to foster sustainable well-being, prevent burnout, and ensure we are the best versions of ourselves, both professionally and personally.

Before the raid, I had developed a consistent routine of pausing my week and having an evening of care, TV, wine, and snacks. As I mentioned earlier, Thursday night was my intentional self-care night as I watched TGIT (Thank God It's Thursday, several shows developed by Chicago native Shonda Rhimes). All that changed after February 21, 2019.

One day, Alicia, my dear therapist, was looking at me and listening to me talk about all I had to do and all I had to hold together. Here I was fighting the City of Chicago with a lawsuit that was stuck in court. I was fighting for reform through the suit and through talking with the media and researching all the other wrongful raids that had impacted innocent people. I was also working my job at the hospital and getting Café Social Work started to fulfill my dream of having a service to help other women social workers, particularly underserved Black women. I had a lot going on. I was spinning many plates in the air and trying my best not to let any fall and crash.

Alicia, in her kind, tender way, asked me: What would happen if things did fall apart? What would happen if those plates crashed?

I looked at her and thought for a moment. I had no answer. Well, actually my answer was: *I can't allow that to happen*. I couldn't imagine anything breaking or stopping or not being carried by me. I had so much going on that I had no plan B. I was fueled by my passion to get this thing right. I had inadvertently taken on the proverbial weight of the world because I was so determined. My resilience had become a stumbling block, I can now admit. But at the time, I could not see it that way.

This realization with Alicia led me to a deeper understanding of the need for self-care. (See? Therapy is worth its weight in gold!) I had heard the word before. I am a licensed clinical social worker and had doled out the advice to others. You've got to take care of yourself, I'd say. I even told this to my clients I worked with at the hospital. In my mind, I understood the concept of self-care. I truly did. The idea that you must take care of yourself before you can take care of others was something I had heard countless times throughout my life. The analogy is simple: you put on your own oxygen mask first, just like flight attendants on airplanes instruct parents to do before they help their children. The logic is sound, the message clear. I could grasp the importance of it all. It made sense in theory.

Understanding a concept intellectually is one thing, but living it out in practice is something else entirely. There's a stark difference between knowing you need self-care and actually making it an active part of your life. I had come to a crossroads—a point in my life where I could no longer deny that I wasn't practicing what I preached. Mentally, I was aware that I wasn't caring for myself, but I didn't fully recognize the dangers of neglecting my own well-being until the toll it began to take on my life became impossible to ignore.

I had been through an unthinkable trauma—the kind of experience that shakes you to your very core. My run-in with the Chicago Police Department had not only left me scarred but also shaken my trust in the very systems that are meant to protect us. I sought therapy, and I even took medication for a while, but these were temporary solutions. What was missing was a sustained, everyday practice of self-care. I was constantly running, working, building, and fighting—not just for myself but also for justice. I was advocating for change, using my voice to speak for others who couldn't. But in doing so, I neglected to ask the most important question: "Who is taking care of me?"

I understood that self-care was essential, but I failed to see how it was something I needed to prioritize daily. I was emotionally and mentally exhausted, constantly moving from one task to the next without taking time to truly nourish myself. I was spending all my energy fighting for the rights of others, speaking out against injustice, and seeking healing for the trauma I had experienced. But I was forgetting to take a breath, to check in with myself, to slow down and allow myself the grace I so readily offered others.

It wasn't until I reached this breaking point—this realization—that I understood the depth of the issue. I was surviving, but I wasn't thriving. I was running on fumes, hoping to hold it all together for the sake of others, while secretly falling apart inside. The daily grind, the push for justice, the need to keep moving forward—it all began to take its toll. I couldn't sustain it any longer without taking the time to care for my own mental, emotional, and physical well-being.

So I had to ask myself: *How could I be the change I wanted to see in the world if I couldn't first change how I was treating myself?* It was a wake-up call, an invitation to slow down and really prioritize my health, my peace, and my healing. I had spent so much time trying to fix the world around me that I failed to see the importance of fixing myself first. I had neglected to nourish my soul, to process my emotions, to give myself permission to heal.

Self-care, I realized, wasn't just about taking breaks or scheduling a spa day. It was about creating space for myself to breathe, to reflect, and to replenish. It was about developing daily practices—such as meditation, exercise, or simply allowing myself to feel my feelings without judgment—that would help me reconnect with my own sense of worth. Only then would I be able to continue the work I needed to do for others, with the strength and clarity to move forward.

It wasn't easy and didn't happen overnight, but I began to understand that self-care isn't a one-time fix—it's a commitment, an ongoing practice. I've learned that taking care of myself doesn't make me weak or selfish. It makes me stronger, more resilient, and better able to handle the challenges life throws at me. It means that I can keep showing up—not just for the world but also for myself.

After getting to an understanding that I had not been caring for myself, I made a change. It didn't happen immediately—change rarely does—but I got to thinking: *What would I do if things fell apart?* I was not God. I was not superwoman. I couldn't control all of these outcomes, I knew that. But why was I acting like things depended solely on me? Why was I allowing my natural tendencies to always get it done?

If you're anything like me—or see even a glimpse of this attitude in your life—I invite you to ask yourself some hard questions; you may activate the help of a trusted therapist or friend to really think through some of these questions. I'm going to dive into some historical and traditional reasons we keep going without taking care of ourselves, but I do hope you will find your own answer so you can fix this before it's too late. I hope you can find the joy and meaning in caring for yourself even as you continue your healing journey and keep fighting and advocating for what is just.

Socialization

Historically, Black women in particular have thought that we always have to take care of things. Even in slavery, we stood by and held it together as men (and of course some women too) were beaten and treated horrifically. We learned how to do things at an early age; we cooked and cleaned, and some of us worked in the field even while pregnant. We cared for the children, grooming them to mind their manners and respect those in charge of our lives. Even when we were liberated, we held on to the attitude that because we were the backbone of the family, we had to keep it together. We were socialized to believe this because it was beneficial to those we took care of; it helped the property owner's bottom line for Black women to have this mindset. There was no room for mistakes or a breakdown. Those who were victims of mental illnesses and could not keep up were seen as weak and damaged and were cast aside.

Even if their ancestors were not enslaved, most women have been conditioned to be caregivers. We put others' needs in front of ours, because we think that is what we're supposed to do. We think that things will literally fall apart if we are not there or if we do not always put others first. What choice do we have? Keep everything moving and care for others at all costs, or be seen as a selfish slacker?

What's wrong with taking a break? What's wrong with saying, "I'm not capable of carrying this load right now. My mental health is not optimal, and I just can't"? Can we normalize not being able to hold it together all the time? Can we find a way to give grace to ourselves and admit that things don't have to have our hands all over them to get done? Someone else can pick it up or not. Life will go on, dear woman. You are not the center of the universe, and you're not responsible for holding up this world.

Try it: Say no. Let one—or two or three—things go. See what happens. Breathe deeply and don't worry about it. Watch the outcome. But more important, watch how you feel. It will take practice to take your hands off everything, but you will and can get used to it. Your body will thank you.

Shame

Along with our idea that we *can* do it all and that we *have to* do it all, there is a sense of shame when we just can't do it. We have internalized the message that everything is up to us or it won't get done, so when we can't or don't do everything, we shudder in shame. We even pass judgment on to others. We disparage the woman who doesn't show up all the time. We whisper about the one who misses too many meetings or isn't signing up for the committee. We look down on those who do not work forty-plus hours per week—clocking in early and staying late—and pick up the family's responsibilities. We secretly compare how much we've done to what others have done, thinking busyness means productivity and productivity is our badge of honor. We think other women are pampered and selfish when we see them taking a break, going to a spa, resting outside with a cup of coffee or tea, or embracing a hobby rather than working for a cause.

I hope we can break these unhealthy attitudes. I hope we can inspire and encourage ourselves as well as our sisters to normalize self-care, to normalize doing what brings you joy, whether that requires extra money or not. Self-care could mean taking a vacation (without work), cooking your favorite meal at a leisurely pace, knitting, crocheting, exercising, sleeping, or anything else that nourishes your soul.

Some of these tasks are things we have to do as a part of life (eat, sleep, exercise), but when we do them as a part of self-care, we nurture not only our bodies but also our spirit. That is the difference, in my opinion, between self-care and just completing a task. When I dance, my spirit feels free. Although dancing is exercise, when it's done with my favorite music and perhaps in the company of my favorite people, it isn't just exercise. Dancing this way feeds my soul. It calls to memory freedom and love and joy.

Sometimes routine activities can become self-care. I've learned to do breathwork while walking my dog. Instead of reviewing all the things that have gone wrong in my day, I try to focus on my breathing exercises. Inhaling fresh air for a period of time and then exhaling that air for a longer period is healthy and restorative not only for my body but also for my emotional state. Breathwork is free, but it needs to be intentional. Taking care of myself also means taking my intentional breaths instead of always rushing off to my next task. I can do breathwork even while doing necessary tasks in my day. (See the resources section for a website that provides more instructions for breathwork.)

I do believe in creating time away from work through vacations. Even when I need to stay home, I plan my time away from my computer. I binge-watch TV shows. I pray and listen to my worship music. Some women enjoy journaling, where they write their thoughts and feelings in a book. Reviewing those thoughts regularly can also help you track your growth on a healing journey or even on a journey toward better self-care. Journaling can be a way of setting goals and reviewing how far you've come and what other improvements you'd like to institute.

One final thought on self-care is to be gentle with yourself. As women, we can be our toughest critics. It's one of the reasons many of us don't think we deserve self-care. We don't think we are worth the time and intentionality self-care requires. If at the very least you change that message in your mind, that in itself can be helpful. Just because you are here, a child of God, you deserve self-care. You deserve to care for the person God created you to be. The Bible speaks of God resting after creating the world in six days: "By the seventh day God had finished the work he had been doing; so on the seventh day he rested from all his work. Then God blessed the seventh day and made it holy, because on it he rested from all the work of creating that he had done" (Genesis 2:2–3).

I doubt that God was tired and needed the rest. I believe God wanted to enjoy all of God's creation and take a break to sit back and review it. I believe that rest day is holy and sacred.

I believe rest itself is holy and sacred and should be honored. Even as I had to slowly challenge myself to take better care of myself and be OK with some things falling apart, I had to learn how to revere rest and make it a priority in my life.

To be honest, it's an ongoing task. Resting doesn't come naturally to me, but I do know I deserve to enjoy rest. I deserve to take care of myself, and I will keep practicing being gentle with myself, scheduling breaks and actually taking them, and doing the things that bring my spirit joy. I'm still looking for those things, and I've pressed repeat on the ones I have found. Will you join me in this quest for radical self-care?

You, too, deserve it.

EPILOGUE

A LETTER TO CHICAGO

DEAR CHICAGO,

Why are we invisible to you? Why is it that women and children—the most vulnerable among us—go unseen in your eyes?

Why do you turn away when wrong raids shatter our communities? When White officers storm into our homes without valid warrants, without justification, treating us as if we were less than human, unworthy of dignity and respect—why is your response silence?

Why do your leaders, who promised to represent and protect us all, stay quiet and allow our suffering to continue? Why do they let us become casualties of a system that claims to serve but so often only harms?

Why do you continue to shield the officers who violated us—who violated the sanctity of our homes, who tore apart our lives—instead of holding them accountable? Is it because they are protected by the same system that has always protected itself, while abandoning people like us, people who look like us?

Where is your responsibility? Where is your humanity?

I have asked myself these questions again and again: Why are we invisible to you? Why do you refuse to see us—to see me—as a woman worthy of justice, of healing, of respect?

Is it because my skin is brown? Is it because I carry the melanin that runs deep in my veins, making me a target before I even speak, before I even act, before I even try to live my life?

Since slavery, my beautiful brown skin has been a symbol of both power and oppression. My ancestors were sold on auction blocks like cattle, their worth determined by the color of their skin and their ability to serve. They were forced to nurse children who weren't their own, to endure pain and hardship just to survive another day. And today it seems that nothing has changed. My body, my existence, my voice are still marginalized, still silenced, and I am still treated as if I am invisible.

The weight of this history is not lost on me. You see, I know that my fight is not just my fight—it is also a continuation of the fight that has been going on for centuries. It is the fight of every Black woman, every person of color, who has ever been treated as less than, as invisible. It is the fight of every ancestor who cried out for justice but was met with silence, just as I have been.

The officers who raided my home did not see me. They didn't see my pain, my fear, or my humanity. They didn't see the trauma they inflicted on me, the terror they caused. To them, I was simply a name on a piece of paper, a target in a city full of targets, a statistic to be ignored and erased. To them, I was nothing but a body to be controlled, a life to be shattered.

And when I tried to speak up, when I tried to tell my story, when I tried to demand accountability, I was met with resistance, with silence, with more of the same. My pain was dismissed. My suffering was disregarded. The system that should have protected me, that should have stood up for me, chose to protect those who harmed me. But I am here to tell you that I will not be silenced. I will not be invisible. I refuse to be forgotten. I refuse to let my story be erased just like the stories of countless others who have been treated as though their lives don't matter. You can try to bury me under your indifference, under your complacency, but I will rise. I will continue to fight, not just for myself but for everyone who has been mistreated, ignored, and made invisible by the system that should protect them.

I know this fight is not easy. I know that change does not come overnight. But how can you continue to ignore the cries of the people? How can you continue to allow these injustices to happen without taking a stand? The system that protects police officers who have done harm to innocent civilians is a system that is broken, a system that needs to be rebuilt. And yet I am still here—still fighting, still pushing, still refusing to be invisible.

The trauma I have endured, the pain I carry with me every day, is not something I can just forget. It is not something I can just sweep under the rug. And yet the City of Chicago continues to act as if my pain, my suffering, and the suffering of so many others doesn't matter. You continue to act as if we are invisible, as if our lives don't count.

But I see you, Chicago. I see you for what you are. I see the systems that protect those who cause harm. I see the complacency that allows these injustices to continue. And I will not be silent. I will not go away. I will continue to fight for the justice we all deserve, for the change we all need.

You may have tried to make me invisible. You may have tried to erase my story, to silence my voice. But I will not be silenced. I will not be erased. I will stand here, and I will fight for what is right. And I will continue to fight until my voice is heard, until my story is told, until justice is served.

As I reflect on your rich history as the third-largest city in the United States, Chicago holds a place of prominence—in the world. And much like my ancestors, I migrated from the South in search of a better life. Black people across the Jim Crow South boarded trains and hitched rides to find a better place, a sort of promised land where factory jobs replaced the cotton field amid a landscape of opportunity. Optimistic, weary, and tired folks from Mississippi, Arkansas, Louisiana, and other Southern spots looked to Chicago as a mecca, a place where Black people could live out their dreams of freedom.

Former plantation workers took shifts at factories, moved in with family members, and worked hard for a better life in what they assumed would be a better city. While that "better" is questionable at times, the Great Migration was beneficial not only for the migrants from the South. It also shaped Chicago in various ways—such as through blues, jazz, and gospel music, giving us talents like Muddy Waters from Mississippi and Mahalia Jackson from Louisiana. The Great Migration also offered new discoveries and created the "Black Metropolis" of Bronzeville, the home of Johnson Publishing Company,

Supreme Life Insurance Company, and other important pillars of Black life.

And we can't forget about the women. Women were and continue to be major contributors to Chicago's greatness. The city shaped Bessie Coleman, the first Black woman to earn a pilot's license. Ida B. Wells, kicked out of Memphis for her reporting and anti-lynching crusade, landed in Chicago, where she worked for women's rights and wrote to make the wrong right. Oprah Winfrey's morning show turned into an international phenomenon from her anchor desk in the Windy City. Chicago is also the place our first African American First Lady discovered who she was and all she could become. Chicago is that city. Great and troubled, mixed together in a metropolis of rich, poor, and those in between.

As Wells once wrote, "The way to right wrongs is to turn the light of truth upon them." I hear her, and I too have picked up that torch to shed that light.

As I peruse the roster of great Chicago women, I can't help but think about Mamie Till-Mobley, whose courage, even in the midst of grief and trauma, sparked the civil rights movement. Although the specific tragedy that was thrust upon her son happened in Mississippi, Till was a resident of Chicago. His mother remained a Chicagoan until her death in 2003. And it was in this city that John H. Johnson made the critical decision to feature her son's maimed body in *Jet* magazine. When people saw those photos, they not only reacted with outrage but also demanded change. Chicago served as the headquarters of this iconic movement in Black history.

During my rabid search for any information on what happened to me and what happened to others in botched raids, I ran across the story of Fred Hampton, which led to my meeting with his wife and son.

In 1969—one year before I was born—FBI officers, assisted by the Chicago Police Department, raided Hampton's home, also on the West Side of Chicago. They fired more than ninety bullets into the apartment where Black Panther Party members were staying. They shot and killed Hampton and Mark Clark while critically wounding four other party members. Hampton's fiancée lay next to him in bed; she was eight months pregnant with their son.

Hampton, a mere twenty-one years old at the time of his death, had been an outspoken and dynamic leader of the Black Panther Party, serving as the Illinois chapter chairman. As part of his position, he had created a pact among Chicago's most powerful street gangs, creating an alliance across racial lines that promised to advocate against poverty, racism, corruption, police brutality, substandard housing, and other systemic atrocities impacting poor people in the city and nation. His actions posed a threat to this country; his voice and his intelligence posed a threat to a system set on keeping Black and Brown people in "their place." Hampton became a target, and his life was snatched from us through a raid where police kicked down the door and fired shotguns and machine guns.

Fred Hampton's son, Fred Hampton Jr., the child who was in his mother's womb as she lay next to Hampton during the raid, miraculously lived, as his mother was not severely hurt during the raid by the nearly one hundred shots fired. Fred Hampton Jr.'s mom is rarely spoken of in our history, but she too was a Black woman harmed by the Chicago Police Department. I want to call her name here so we may remember yet another Black woman forever changed by a raid: Akua Njeri. This sister too was a Black woman harmed by a system that was supposed to be set up to serve and protect her. The imprints of that night remain on her heart, mind, and soul, yet like me, she kept moving and emerged with a stronger and more focused purpose. She continues the fight to remind us all of Fred Hampton and his work for justice; she has written a book and consulted on stories about Hampton. Akua and her son Fred have been comforting allies with me on my journey to seek reform. They've often showed up to be by my side. It's reassuring to stand by those who understand this type of trauma on a personal level. While it doesn't make it better because it is an offense against us, it does make me feel seen and heard.

Chicago has a history of hurting the very people who are trying to help her. Fred Hampton Jr. was born into this tragic scene. In utero, he was traumatized. His mother was traumatized just because of her partner's desire to bring unity to a city that had treated Black and Brown citizens separately and not equally.

It is unfortunate that in Chicago many Black and Brown people—men and women—have a shared traumatic experience, much of which has been fostered by the inequalities and injustices of this great city. While these women and men may never show up on CBS News, we walk beside them daily as they move from the bus stops to the El and dodge in and out of traffic, suffering in silence, trying to move past what has been thrust upon them.

I write this book for those women and men impacted by the trauma we don't ever speak about. I write this book to share that healing is available. Even more so, I write this book to share that we have a voice, and whether or not we all can use our voices, some of us, like me, are speaking up for all of us.

We need reform. We need to be seen and respected. The police can still do their jobs while caring for the citizens. Caring. Seeing. Doing the extra work to ensure the safety of the innocent. Research. Reform. Respect. That's what we ask; it's what we demand.

I, like you, was born a child of God. "[God] created my inmost being; you knit me together in my mother's womb. I praise you because I am fearfully and wonderfully made; your works are wonderful, I know that full well."

To my core, I believe those words, first penned by David, King of Israel, in Psalm 139:13–14. I'm glad I grew up in an era where Black people were no longer legally considered three-fifths of a human. I still live in a world where Black and Brown people can be bypassed, treated as less than human, and not given the proper care and consideration by those in charge of our safety. But I was born at a time when a grandmother poured into my spirit, reminding me who I was and what I was called to do. I was born at a time when resources—thank God—are readily available for those of us desiring to push past the pain and seek the necessary help to heal. I was born at a time when I can take my voice to my local government, my state government, and even my national government. As Esther's relative Mordecai reminds her in the Old Testament story, "Who knows but that [I] have come to [this] position for such a time as this?" (Esther 4:14).

This just may be the time America rights a wrong and creates the reform needed to protect everyone. I might be the vessel God uses to remind people that Black women are not invisible. Black and Brown people are not invisible.

Chicago has been good to me—mostly. It has allowed me to raise my son, have a meaningful career, and serve in a spiritually and socially uplifting church. It's given me world-class entertainment, from free festivals and fireworks to cultural exhibits and amazing food and experiences. Chicago is that city. But there's so much more work Chicago has to do to be that city for all of us. Those who have big voices, those who may not feel comfortable speaking, those who are Black and those who are Brown. Everyone deserves to be able to live in this city and feel safe and protected. It's an unalienable right.

I pray this city can live up to its world-class status. And I pray that every woman, man, or child who has been harmed in some way by the system set up to trap us will also find healing—a healing that leads to change, to hope, to wholeness and a sense of thriving.

Remember: What they meant for evil, God can use for your good!

ACKNOWLEDGMENTS

A HEARTFELT THANK-YOU

WRITING THIS BOOK has been one of the most challenging yet rewarding journeys of my adult life. The process of putting these words on paper has meant reliving the most traumatic experience I have ever endured, over and over again. It has meant peeling back layers of pain, revisiting wounds that I thought had healed, and finding the courage to articulate what once felt impossible to say. There were moments when I felt completely drained—mentally, emotionally, and spiritually. Yet, through it all, I pushed forward. Not by my strength alone, but by the grace of God and the unwavering support of those He placed in my life.

This book is more than just a collection of words; it is a testament to survival, resilience, and transformation. It is evidence of who I was designed to be from the beginning of time. Every page, every paragraph, every sentence reflects a part of my journey—a journey that has tested me, shaped me, and ultimately refined me. And today, you all get to witness that transformation. To God be the glory for all that I am and all that I will continue to be. I am here today, standing strong, because of the Almighty.

But let me be clear—I did not get here on my own. My strength has been sustained by my tribe, by the people who carried me every step of the way, especially when I didn't think I could take another step myself.

Honoring My Grandmother

First and foremost, I am Lucendia's grandbaby. My grandmother was, and still is, my guiding light. She shaped me into the woman I am today, instilling in me the values of perseverance, dignity, and faith. Even though she is no longer physically here, her wisdom and love remain woven into every fiber of my being. Every victory I have, every milestone I reach, is because of the foundation she laid for me. I carry her with me, always.

A Legal Champion and Brother in Christ

I want to express my deepest gratitude to my attorney, Keenan Saulter. This man of God—who started out as my deacon, stepped up as my attorney, covered and protected me like a big brother, and has truly become a beloved friend—was my ram in the bush. None of this happens without him. When I felt lost, overwhelmed, and unheard, he stood firm in my corner, fighting for justice on my behalf. His wisdom, tenacity, and unwavering faith gave me the confidence to stand in my truth, even when the world tried to silence me. Keenan, you are a blessing beyond words, and I will always be grateful for you.

The Visionaries Who Believed in This Book

Huge thanks to my agent and editor, Keely Boving and Katara Washington Patton, who believed in this book before it was even a book. They saw what was to come before I could fully envision it myself. They worked tirelessly to secure the right publishing house and guided me through this process with so much patience, wisdom, and encouragement. Their belief in my story and their commitment to ensuring it was told in the most powerful way possible has been invaluable. Thank you both for walking with me every step of the way.

Special thanks to my therapist, Alicia Troff-Meade. It was during my emptiest moments that she walked alongside me. She always made herself available, even during non-office hours; she never turned me away when I needed her support. I am thankful for her sharing her expertise at the end of most chapters in this book.

I also extend my sincere thanks to my dear friend and fellow church member, Esau McCaulley, who taught me how to write. In the early stages of this journey, when the idea of writing a book felt overwhelming, Esau took the time to coach me through the intricate details of storytelling. He gave me writing assignments, challenged my perspective, and helped me shape my voice in ways I never thought possible. His guidance was instrumental in helping me find the courage to put my truth on paper.

Thank you to Chicago Review Press for believing in my story and being willing to bet on me as an unpolished author. I had a story that needed to be told to the world.

Family—My Lifelong Support System

To my family, who has always stood by me through every season of life—thank you. To my uncle Joe, who helped me to remember the spirit and legacy of Grandma as I wrote this book. To my "cousin crew," my ride-or-dies, my day ones: Danielle, Gabby, Jasmine, Shay, and Mesha. You checked on me daily, lifted me up when I was down, and reminded me who I was when I started to forget.

A special shout-out to my cousin Lawankia, who is no longer with us. Your laughter, love, and spirit remain with me always. I carry your memory in my heart, and I know you are watching over me with pride.

My Spiritual Home and Church Family

To my pastor, Rev. Dr. Charlie Dates, and my entire Progressive Baptist Church family, thank you for being a place of refuge for me. To Rev. Ray, whom I lovingly call "Unc," and to my little brother, Pastor Jamal, and his wife—your prayers, your presence, and your encouragement have meant more to me than words can express.

To my church girls—Joyce, Bernadette, and Michaela—you saw me cry more times than I can count, yet you never wavered. You prayed over me, stood beside me, and lifted me up when I felt like I couldn't go on. Your love and support have been an anchor for me, keeping me grounded in faith, even during my darkest moments.

The Social Work Community and Political Champions

To my social work family, Latesha, Joel, and Kyle, and the National Association of Social Workers–Illinois (NASW-IL), thank you for standing with me. You have been by my side, advocating, organizing, and ensuring that our work extends beyond my personal experience to fight for systemic change.

Stepping into the political arena was never part of my original plan, but I am so grateful for the women and men who stood beside me as I took on this new fight. Alderwoman Maria Hadden and Alderwoman Jeanette Taylor—you both went to battle for me, fighting against city hall and refusing to let my voice be silenced. Your courage and determination have inspired me beyond measure.

To Representative Kam Buckner, Representative Kelly Cassidy, and the many other state legislators who stepped up—not because it was convenient or politically beneficial, but because it was the right thing to do—thank you. Your support has meant everything.

To the Local and National Media

I extend my deepest gratitude to Dave Savini at CBS2 Chicago, Gayle King at *CBS Mornings* in New York, and every media outlet that shared my story. Your dedication to truth and justice helped bring awareness to a deeply troubling situation. By amplifying my voice, you not only shed light on injustice but also became champions for change. Your relentless pursuit of accountability and fairness has made a profound impact, turning pain into purpose. Thank you for using your platforms to stand for what is right and to give a voice to those who need it most.

To the Countless People Who Stood in Solidarity

Finally, I am deeply, profoundly grateful to every single person who stood with me, whether I know your name or not. To those who prayed for me, wrote letters, called elected officials, attended rallies, and refused to let my story be forgotten—you are the reason this fight has continued.

To every person who saw what happened to me and chose to take action, who spoke out, who amplified my voice when others tried to drown it out—thank you. Your support has reminded me that I am not alone in this journey. It has reminded me that even in the face of injustice, there is power in community.

A Final Word of Gratitude

This book is not just my story—it is also a testament to the resilience of so many who have suffered in silence. It is a call to action, a demand for change, and a beacon of hope for those still fighting.

A special note to my dear friend, Peter Mendez: You have been a guiding light on this journey, showing me the way with your kindness and allowing me to be a part of your journey. Meeting you has been a true blessing, and I am deeply grateful for the bond we share. I carry that with me every step of the way. I have no doubt that incredible things await you in the future, and I look forward to seeing all that you will accomplish. Thank you for being a part of this journey with me.

I never wanted to be in this position, but now that I am here, I embrace it fully. And I do so knowing that I am surrounded by an incredible community of love, faith, and unwavering support.

From the depths of my heart, thank you. Thank you for believing in me. Thank you for fighting with me. Thank you for reminding me that even after the darkest of nights, the sun will rise again.

RESOURCES

Finding a Counselor or Therapist

The National Alliance of Mental Illness (NAMI) describes several different types of mental health professionals who may assist in helping you meet your healing goals. They include:

Psychologists: These professionals hold a doctoral degree in clinical psychology or another specialty such as counseling or education. They can evaluate your mental health by using interviews, evaluations, and testing. They can provide individual therapy or group therapy. They are licensed by their state's board.

Counselors, Clinicians, Therapists: These professionals have master's-level degrees and are trained to evaluate your mental health. They use a variety of therapeutic techniques for treatment. Their licensure needs and processes vary by state.

Clinical Social Workers: These professionals are trained to evaluate your mental health and are also trained in case management and advocacy services. They have a master's degree in social work and can have licensures as Licensed Independent Social Workers, Licensed Clinical Social Workers, or Academy of Certified Social Workers.

Psychiatrists: These professionals are medical doctors who have received psychiatric training. They can diagnose mental health conditions as well as prescribe and monitor medications and therapy. They are licensed physicians in each state they practice in.

Psychiatric or Mental Health Nurse Practitioners: These professionals can provide diagnosis and therapy for mental health conditions or substance use disorders. In some states, they may prescribe and monitor medications. They are licensed as nurses in their particular state but may also have additional licensure.

Tammy Lewis Wilborn, PhD, recommends utilizing the following websites to find out more about therapy and maybe even finding a therapist:

Therapy for Black Girls
https://therapyforblackgirls.com/
The mission of this community, which includes a podcast, is "to be seen, to be heard, and to be understood." The description on the site goes on to say: "So often the stigma surrounding mental health issues and therapy prevents Black women from taking the step of seeing a therapist. This space was developed to present mental health topics in a way that feels more accessible and relevant."

Psychology Today
https://www.psychologytoday.com/us
This site includes Find a Therapist, a searchable directory for therapists by zip code and city. Don't forget to check your insurance benefits for mental wellness support that may be offered for free or at a drastically reduced cost.

Practices and Techniques

Breathwork for Beginners
https://health.clevelandclinic.org/breathwork

Books I Used

***What Happened to You? Conversations on Trauma, Resilience, and Healing* by Oprah Winfrey and Bruce Perry (2021):** This book addresses how being from a minority group within a majority group is a traumatizing experience in itself.

***The Body Keeps the Score: Brain, Mind, and Body in the Healing of Trauma* by Bessel Van der Kolk, MD (2014):** Trauma affects not only those who are directly exposed to it but also those around them.

***Detours: The Unpredictable Path to Your Destiny* by Tony Evans (2017):** Alicia and I walked through some of these chapters during my therapy sessions. "[There] are times when God seeks to mold us into the character He can use for the good works He has prepared. That's not always fun. Sometimes it hurts. It's often longer than any of us wish. But God will accomplish His desired result, if you allow Him. It's only when we fuss, fight, and complain that our detours drag on longer than necessary."

Power Moves: Ignite Your Confidence and Become a Force **by Sarah Jakes (2024):** Confidence is an inside job, but becoming a force is when your confidence gives you the courage to be a solution to what is happening around you.

Other Books on Healing

Navigating the Blues: Where to Turn When Worry, Anxiety, or Depression Steals Your Hope **by Katara Washington Patton (2023):** This 90-day devotion gives you small doses of help and encouragement to keep going.

Black Woman Grief: A Guide to Hope and Wholeness **by Natasha Smith (2025):** I've referenced this book several times. It gives voice to so much of what women, especially Black women, have experienced for too long in this country.

Playing a New Game: A Black Woman's Guide to Being Well and Thriving in the Workplace **by Tammy Lewis Wilborn, PhD (2025):** The author of this book so graciously spoke with us about Black women and therapy and recovering from trauma. Her advice is quoted throughout *Past the Pain*.

Her Rites: A Sacred Journey for the Mind, Body, and Soul **by Christy Angelle Bauman, PhD (2024):** The author of this book also talked to me about trauma recovery and the various work she does to help women achieve wholeness.

Resources for Helping Survivors of Trauma

Micro vs. Macro Social Work

https://online.yu.edu/wurzweiler/blog/micro-vs-macro-social-work

This article from Yeshiva University gives a detailed overview of micro versus macro social work. For anyone considering entering the field or who just wants to learn more about the field, this is a great place to begin.

Trauma-Informed Care

https://www.safeaustin.org/supporting-survivors-a-trauma-informed-approach/

This site lists and defines five principles of trauma-informed care. The article may prove helpful to those working in the field and includes discussions on safety, choice, collaboration, trustworthiness, and empowerment.

Helping Someone Else with Trauma

https://www.mind.org.uk/information-support/types-of-mental-health-problems/trauma/for-friends-and-family/

This site is filled with various resources and good information on trauma-informed care.

I AM HER Foundation

https://iamher21.com/

This site introduces I AM HER, the not-for-profit foundation I created as a result of my healing journey. I desire to make sure Black women in particular have the resources they need to become whole and healthy. I want every Black woman and girl to know their voices will no longer be silenced by shame, guilt, and injustices of this world.

My pastor, Rev. Dr. Charlie Dates (I call him Pastor Charlie), offers these comments to pastors and others working with survivors who have endured severe trauma:
Your immediate questions should be about the person's physical, spiritual, and emotional well-being. First, ensure they are in a physically safe space, then provide counseling and support. Over the long term, it's crucial to offer sustained care. Congregants need your phone calls, your support, and your attention. In addition, pastors should engage political, judicial, and law enforcement branches to ensure that the trauma is addressed for the greater good of the person and their community.

One of the pastors at my church, Rev. Raynard Hawkins, assisted me tremendously immediately after the raid. He offers the following to anyone helping someone in the midst of trauma, particularly when armed police officers are involved:
I would strongly recommend *not* to amplify at ground zero the misdeed of perpetrators (in Anjanette Young's case, ironically, the police). That's not the time. The job of the first responder is simply to give the best comfort and care as possible. Help the victim put it back together for the moment; the time will come for accountability. Anjanette's case and fight, for me, has never been about the revenge; it's about the reform and the reckoning.

NOTES

All Bible quotes are from the New International Version (NIV) translation.

1. The Night That Changed Everything

Common causes of trauma: "Signs of Emotional Trauma in Adults," Fort Behavioral Health, December 29, 2022, https://fortbehavioral.com/addiction-recovery-blog/signs-of-emotional-trauma-in-adults/.

2. The Morning After: Taking Baby Steps

"expectations that we are selfless": Tammy Lewis Wilborn, *Playing a New Game: A Black Woman's Guide to Being Well and Thriving in the Workplace* (New York: Balance, 2022), 51.

"Reacting to stress in unhealthy ways": "Stress and High Blood Pressure: What's the Connection?," Mayo Clinic, November 23, 2024, https://www.mayoclinic.org/diseases-conditions/high-blood-pressure/in-depth/stress-and-high-blood-pressure/art-20044190.

consider your immediate needs: Wilborn, *Playing a New Game*, 101.

"Remember, the first thing": Wilborn, *Playing a New Game*, 92.

3. Breonna Taylor: Triggers, Grief, and Healing

"there is a ton of grief": Christy Angelle Bauman, *Her Rites: A Sacred Journey for the Mind, Body, and Soul* (New York: Convergent Books, 2024), 85.

"your nervous system remembering": Hillary L. McBride, *The Wisdom of Your Body: Finding Healing, Wholeness, and Connection Through Embodied Living* (Grand Rapids, MI: Brazos, 2021), 68.

"The challenge of recovery": Bessel van der Kolk, *The Body Keeps the Score*, quoted in *Black Woman Grief : A Guide to Hope and Wholeness* by Natasha Smith (Downers Grove, IL: IVP, 2025), 95.

"breathing techniques that intentionally channel": "Breathwork for Beginners: What to Know and How to Get Started," Cleveland Clinic, May 19, 2023, https://health.clevelandclinic.org/breathwork.

4. A Search for Answers

part of the two-year investigation: *[un]warranted: A CBS 2 News Documentary*, CBS Chicago, YouTube, December 17, 2020, https://www.youtube.com/watch?v=B-JqbRfPAVI.

"Needing and taking medication": Wilborn, *Playing a New Game*, 3.

"Taking medication can be": Wilborn, *Playing a New Game*, 3.

I came across a website: Chicago Gang History, accessed June 20, 2025, https://chicagoganghistory.com/.

5. Lucendia's Grandbaby: The Fight Was in My DNA

She talks about purpose emerging: Sarah Jakes Roberts, *Power Moves: Ignite Your Confidence & Become a Force* (Nashville: W Publishing, 2024), 91.

6. Justice, Support, and the Church

"Community is one of the greatest helps": Quantrilla Ard, foreword to *Black Woman Grief: A Guide to Hope and Wholeness* by Natasha Smith (Downers Grove, IL: IVP, 2025), 4.

"reducing the impact of trauma": Katie Schultz, Lauren B. Cattaneo, Chiara Sabina, et al., "Key Roles of Community Connectedness in Healing from Trauma," *Psychology of Violence* 6, no. 2 (January 2016): 42, https://www.researchgate.net/publication/290210427_Key_roles_of_community_connectedness_in_healing_from_trauma.

7. Social Worker Turned Activist: Helping Others Can Help You Heal

Micro-level social work focuses: "Micro vs. Macro Social Work: What Is the Difference?," Yeshiva University, April 21, 2022, https://online.yu.edu/wurzweiler/blog/micro-vs-macro-social-work.

8. I Am a Testimony

"It is okay to get support": Wilborn, *Playing a New Game*, 161.

Epilogue: A Letter to Chicago

"The way to right wrongs": Jillian Peprah-Frimpong, "The Way to Right Wrongs: Celebrating the Legacy of Ida B. Wells," New York Public Library, July 16, 2018, https://www.nypl.org/blog/2018/07/16/way-right-wrongs-celebrating-legacy-ida-b-wells.

ABOUT ALICIA TROFF-MEADE

Alicia Troff-Meade is a licensed clinical social worker. She attended the University of Michigan, where she received a BA in psychology, as well as the University of Chicago, where she received her MA in clinical social work. Since 1982, she has worked in several clinical settings including community mental health, Regional Safe Schools, psychiatric inpatient units, and the Cook County Public Guardian Domestic Relations Division. With over forty years of clinical experience, she currently operates a private practice in Oak Park, Illinois, specializing in depression, anxiety, and trauma recovery with an emphasis on dialectical behavioral therapy, internal family systems, and mindfulness.

Her website is www.alicia-meade-psychotherapy.com.